RENATA SALECL is a philosopher and sociologist. She is a visiting professor at BIOS centre at the London School of Economics and at Birkbeck College School of Law. She is also a senior researcher at the Institute of Criminology at the Faculty of Law in Ljubljana, Slovenia and a recurring visiting professor at Cardozo School of Law in New York. Her previous books include On Anxiety (Routledge, 2004) and have been translated into ten languages.

BIG IDEAS

General editor: Lisa Appignanesi

As the twenty-first century moves through its tumultuous first decade, we need to think about our world afresh. It's time to revisit not only politics, but our passions and preoccupations, and our ways of seeing the world. The Big Ideas series challenges people who think about these subjects to think in public, where soundbites and polemics too often provide sound and fury but little light. These books stir debate and will continue to be important reading for years to come.

Other titles in the series include:

THE TYRANNY OF
CHOICE

Renata Salecl

P
PROFILE BOOKS

This paperback edition published in 2011

First published in Great Britain in 2010 by
PROFILE BOOKS LTD
3A Exmouth House
Pine Street
London EC1R 0JH
www.profilebooks.com

Copyright © Renata Salecl, 2010, 2011

3 5 7 9 10 8 6 4 2

Typeset in Minion by MacGuru Ltd
info@macguru.org.uk
Printed and bound by CPI Group
(UK) Ltd, Croydon, CR0 4YY

The moral right of the author has been asserted.

A CIP catalogue record for this book is available from the
British Library.

ISBN 978 1 84668 186 8
eISBN 978 1 84765 226 3

MIX
Paper from
responsible sources
FSC® C020852

CONTENTS

INTRODUCTION

Browsing through the self-help section of a New York bookshop, I came across a book entitled *All About Me*. The book was mostly blank. On each page there was only a question or two about the reader's likes and dislikes, memories and plans for the future – nothing more.

These empty spaces perfectly illustrate the dominant ideology of the developed world: the individual is the ultimate master of his or her life, free to determine every detail. In today's consumer society we are not only required to choose between products: we are asked to see our whole lives as one big composite of decisions and choices.

During a single train journey, for example, I was reminded many times that I am free to make whatever I want out of my life. An advertisement for a university encouraged me to 'Become what you want to be'. A beer company urged, 'Be yourself'. A travel company exhorted, 'Life – book now'. The cover of *Cosmopolitan* read, 'Become yourself – only a better version'. When I used a Chase Manhattan cash machine, the screen told me: 'Your choice. Your Chase'. Even in post-Communist countries, advertising tells us that we should endlessly be deciding what kind of life to live. In Slovenia a lingerie company put up huge advertising hoardings asking, 'What woman do you want to be today?' A Bulgarian mobile phone company uses the logo 'It's your voice', and its Croatian counterpart repeats the mantra: 'Be yourself!'

Becoming oneself seems to be no easy task. A quick look at the bestseller lists suggests that people are spending a lot of time and money learning how to become themselves. *Change Your Thought: Change Yourself, You: The Owner's Manual, Now Discover Your Strengths* and *Reposition Yourself* – each offers a new strategy for redefining one's entire life. Internet astrology sites advertise free insight into the 'real you', television ads encourage a total body makeover and in every area of private and public life there are coaches available to help one achieve the ideal lifestyle.

All this advice, however, does not necessarily bring contentment; instead, it can actually increase one's anxiety and insecurity.

One magazine editor, Jennifer Niesslein, decided to try to resolve all the problems in her life, using only the advice offered in a variety of self-help books that promised to help her find happiness and fulfilment. In her book *Practically Perfect in Every Way* Niesslein describes how, after two years of following advice on how to lose weight, declutter her house, be a better parent and a better partner and find more serenity in her overall existence, she started suffering from serious panic attacks.[1] She found herself *less* contented, not more. Not only were all these attempts at self-improvement taking up all her time, but she wasn't enjoying what she had achieved: a spotless kitchen, three home-cooked meals a day and the new communication skills that she had mastered. Even the weight that she had lost through strenuous exercise came back within a few months. When it was all over,

Niesslein explained why she thought people follow these books rather than attempting to change on their own terms: 'I think we feel responsible for so much in our lives. There's jobs, kids, the responsibility for your marriage. If you can turn to someone else and they'll tell you what to do, it's comforting.'[2]

How is it that in the developed world this increase in choice, through which we can supposedly customise our lives and make them perfect leads not to more satisfaction but rather to greater anxiety, and greater feelings of inadequacy and guilt? And why is it that in order to alleviate this anxiety people are willing to follow random bits of advice from marketing people or horoscopes, take beauty tips from the cosmetics industry, be guided by economic forecasts from financial advisers and accept relationship advice from the writers of self-help books? Given that more and more people defer to these so-called experts, it would seem that we are increasingly eager actually to have the burden of choice taken away from us.

People are often trapped into a vicious circle when they try to improve their lives with the help of experts. For example, some psychoanalysts have observed a particular kind of obsessive behaviour among the followers of the 'FLYlady.com' self-help website. (FLY stands for 'Finally Loving Yourself'), whose readers are encouraged to keep a journal of their daily tasks and to follow detailed advice on how to de-clutter their space, their bodies, their emotions and their relationships. The site's users would complain to psychoanalysts that they were constantly failing to accomplish the tasks they had been set or that the list of tasks they wanted to complete grew ever longer. Some would even behave as though their whole life was a list of achievements that had to be fulfilled: work on a particular assignment, lose a certain amount of weight, get married by a certain age, have a child, build the perfect home. Yet complaining about their inadequacy, however self-induced, seemed to bring a particular pleasure of its own.

These forms of self-torture go hand in hand with attempts to pursue ever new forms of enjoyment. Post-industrial capitalist ideology tends to treat the individual as someone for whom enjoyment is without limit. She is portrayed as someone who can endlessly push back the boundaries of pleasure, constantly satisfying her ever-expanding desires. Paradoxically, however, many people do not find satisfaction in a society seemingly without boundaries, and often swerve instead onto a path of self-destruction. Unfettered consumption tends to lead people to consume themselves; with self-harm, anorexia, bulimia and addictions being only the most obvious forms.

When the current economic crisis began in 2008, it seemed at first as though choice had been replaced by restraint, happiness by gloom and individual freedom by the desire for an authority figure to take charge and put things right. Standard-bearers such as the *Financial Times* ran articles on the gloomy economic situation with headlines such as 'A Borrowed Tomorrow'; 'Payback Time' and 'Wall Street Drowns Its Sorrows'. An analysis of society at large began with a call for a reality check, a 'clean break'. A 'sense of irrationality' was said to be hovering over everything. Even in articles on the arts a new fatalistic discourse seemed to be emerging. The question 'How To Survive The End Of "Civilization"' was answered by recourse to the 'Master Of Balance And Harmony', the 'Voice Of The Future' or 'Songs Of Simplicity'.[3] But as soon as there appeared a glimmer of hope that the crisis might not mean total economic meltdown, the idea of choice re-emerged as the powerful ideological tool of consumer society. This time it was wrapped in discussions as to whether prosperity truly increases happiness and whether conspicuous consumption was the best way for people to spend their free time. But these very ideas about simplifying life became enmeshed in another version of choice. The consumer had to choose not to choose and often had to pay for advice on how to do this. Simply throwing things away or donating them to someone else was not an option: advice was needed on how to do it.

This shift in the perception of prosperity, however, did not happen overnight. It is not that people suddenly woke up one day and saw their lives differently. The seeds of the impending economic crisis had been sown some time earlier. Similarly, depression about the ideology of choice had already permeated times of greater exuberance, as is clear from the anxiety and insecurity evident during the last decade of post-industrial capitalism. It is almost as though the crisis represented the fulfilment of a desire, only partially given voice for some limit to the plethora of choice available during wealthier years, as well as the concomitant release from the pressure created by it. The crisis even brought a strange, relieved form of enjoyment in some quarters, where a desire for some cap on extravagance – or rather, on the multitudinous possibilities that affluence allowed – had long been felt, though only partially realised. *The New York Times* caught this new puritanical mood by outlining a downsized way to celebrate the holidays in an article entitled 'We're Going to Party Like It's 1929'. The piece suggested how people could hold a decent dinner party on a more modest budget in the midst of the crisis. One socialite featured in the article observed: 'The thing about the recession is, it takes the pressure off … It allows you to strip away all the stuff that's not important and focus on what is: friends, family, togetherness.'[4] Yet the party hosts felt the need to hire an adviser to tell them how to entertain in times of crisis. There was a distinct ambivalence in their wish to give up on the thrills of consumption. They may have wanted to limit their choices, but not too much, and they wanted someone else to do it for them.

The question to be examined here is not simply why people shop, or how they think about their lives, but *why* they embrace the idea of choice, and what is gained and lost when they do. People may worry about the terrorist threat, or new viruses and environmental disasters, but their greatest worries are usually about their own private well-being: their jobs, relationships, finances, their place in the community, the meaning of their lives, or the legacy they will pass on.[5] All of these involve choices. And since we strive for perfection not only in the here and now but also in the future, choices become even harder to make. Choice brings a sense of overwhelming responsibility into play, and this is bound up with a fear of failure, a feeling of guilt and an anxiety that regret will follow if we have made the wrong choice. All this contributes to the tyrannical aspect of choice.

The sociologist Richard Sennett points out:

> One of the oldest usages of the word 'tyranny' in political thought is a synonym for sovereignty. When all matters are referred to a common, sovereign principle or reason, that principle or person tyrannizes the life of a society ... An institution can rule as a single fount of authority; a belief can serve as a single standard for measuring reality.[6]

In the last few decades the idea of choice, as presented in rational choice theory, has become one such tyrannical idea in the developed world.

Rational choice theory presupposes that people think before they act and that they will always seek to maximise the benefits and minimise the costs of any situation. Depending on the prevailing circumstances and given sufficient information, people will thus always choose the option that is in their own best interest. Critics of rational choice theory, however, have pointed out that human beings don't always act in their own interest even when they know what that is. Hence the many instances where people act in a charitable or altruistic manner rather than on the basis of naked self-interest. Psychoanalysis has also shown that people often behave in ways that do not maximise their pleasure and minimise their pain and that they even sometimes derive a strange pleasure from acting against their own well-being. Even if people think that they have the necessary information to make the best choice available, their decision will be heavily influenced by external factors, such as other people, or by internal factors, such as their own unconscious desires and wishes.

In today's society, which glorifies choice and the idea that choice is always in people's interests, the problem is not just the scale of choice available but the manner in which choice is represented. Life choices are described in the same terms as consumer choices: we set out to find the 'right' life as we would to find the right kind of wallpaper or hair conditioner. Today's advice culture presents the search for a spouse as not all that different from the search for a car: first we need to weigh up all the advantages and disadvantages, then we need to secure a prenuptial agreement, mend things if they go wrong and eventually trade in the old model for a new one, before finally getting tired of all the hassle of commitment and deciding to go for a temporary lease agreement.

The issue of choice has been a concern primarily of the middle classes in the developed world. Yet even in poor countries many have been deeply troubled by the contradictions inherent in the ideology of choice. Supposedly now free to make whatever they want out of their lives, in reality they suffer from numerous constraints. People are treated as though they are in a position to make a work of art out of their own lives, shaping every element at will. They are encouraged to act as though they live in an ideal world and as though the choices they make are reversible, while the reality is that their economic circumstances prevent them from having much freedom of choice at all and that one wrong decision can have disastrous consequences. Even in wealthy countries poor people lack the ability to take advantage of the choices on offer to them. In the USA, for example, there are a huge range of treatments and technology to choose from if you have health insurance and can afford them. But without universal healthcare poor people cannot choose even the most basic treatment. And even for those for whom money is not an issue, choice can be a burden and source of confusion: on the one hand, the latest scientific research tells them that their genes have already determined what illnesses they will have and how long they will live; on the other, they are made to feel responsible for their own well-being through their lifestyle choices.

The aim of this book is to explore how the idea of choosing who we want to be and the imperative to 'become yourself' have begun to work against us, making us more anxious and more acquisitive rather than giving us more freedom. Post-industrial capitalism's espousal of the ideology of choice is not a coincidence but rather enables it to perpetuate its dominance. The problem, the French philosopher Luis Althusser suggests, is that we don't notice the forms in which our lives are constructed. Society functions as something obvious, something given, almost natural. In order to understand the hidden imperatives, the codes of being, the secret requirements that philosophers call 'ideologies', we need to remove the veil of obviousness and given-ness. Only then do we notice the bizarre but highly ordered logic that we obey, unthinkingly, in our everyday lives. We may well feel ourselves opposed to 'society' or the 'status quo': however, paradoxically, for a particular ideology to survive, it is not essential that people actively support or believe in it. The crucial thing is that people do not express their disbelief. For them to abide by the majority opinion, all that matters is that they believe it to be true that most of the people around them believe. Ideologies thus thrive on 'belief in the belief of others'. This was perhaps most obvious in former Communist regimes, where most people did not fully believe in the dominant ideology. Citizens reason along the lines of: 'I do not believe in the Party, but there are many, more numerous and powerful than me and those like me (and not only Party apparatchiks) who do, so I will keep in line.' (It now seems that in fact not even many Party apparatchiks were genuine believers in Communism. They were often deeply suspicious of people who went back to the works of the founders of socialism, Marx and Engels.) In the end what held society together was a belief in those fictional others who supposedly did believe and who thus enforced belief.

This logic of belief holds for the idea of choice. We may not think that our choices are limitless or that we are fully capable of determining the direction of our lives and making ourselves whatever we want to be, but we believe that someone else believes in these ideas and so we do not express our disbelief. For the ideology of choice to hold such power in post-industrial society, all that is needed is for people to keep their disbelief to themselves.

In the process of feeling guilty about who we are and working constantly to 'improve' ourselves we lose the perspective necessary to instigate any social change. By working so hard at self-improvement we lose the energy and ability to participate in any form of social change and constantly feel anxious that we are somehow failing.

If we want to relieve this anxiety, we must understand how it has taken hold in the first place and how it works. And if we hope to change the way society functions, we must acknowledge that there are alternatives to the tyranny of choice, which plays such a central role in the ideology of late capitalism. Instead of glorifying rational choice, we need to look at how choices are often made at an unconscious level and how they are influenced by society at large.

In times of economic crisis other questions arise. How do we go from boundless free choice to severely limited choice? How can we go from believing that everything is possible to believing that nothing is possible any longer? How can we forget the promise and face the reality? These questions entwine us in the difficult logic of loss. In the developed world the last decades have created the illusion of an eternal present: the past does not matter, and the future is ours to create. In the midst of this, the reality of loss is occluded. Decisions become ever harder to make when one is perceived as being the master of one's fate, of one's own well-being and the well-being of those close to us: our children, for example. The feeling of regret for decisions that one took, the fear of making another mistake, can become overwhelming. In order to avoid feelings of loss and regret, and a pervasive anxiety, one tries to minimise risk or at least make it predictable. The society that prizes choice relies on the idea that we have to prevent all risk, or at least predict it.

Crisis can be defined as precisely the moment when we lose control – the moment when the world we know is destroyed and we are confronted with the unknown. Whatever its consequences for society, for the individual, such a crisis may be a moment to reassess what really matters. When an economic crisis compels people to save, they are also being forced to consider their desires. To save is to sacrifice desire – or, at least, to defer it. Until recently, the society of choice encouraged immediate gratification and taught us not to defer anything.

But even in the midst of this process, people have formed ever new limits in order to keep their desire alive: they have invented new prohibitions of their own to curb their society's push to enjoyment. This is why I disagree with theories that we live in a society without limits. There is a difference between a society where limits do not exist and an ideology that *depicts* that society as being without limits. While our current ideology, as represented in the media, has played on the limitlessness of enjoyment, the individual still struggles with his or her own prohibitions.

Dostoevsky's character Ivan Karamazov (in *The Brothers Karamazov*) reasons that, if God does not exist, then everything is permissible. The French psychoanalyst

Jacques Lacan reversed this into 'If God does not exist, nothing is permitted any longer', meaning that the loss of belief in an authority that prohibits our actions opens the door not to freedom but rather to the creation of new limits. With the ideology of choice we are confronted by similar reversals. The limitless choices that we are supposed to have in regard to our lives have turned into new prohibitions. Nowadays, however, it is not that these limits are imposed on us by an external authority, such as parents, or teachers, but rather that we create our own prohibitions. And the vast advice/self-help industry also enables us to choose yet further authorities to whom we can delegate the right to limit our choices.

This book will show how misleading the ideology of choice can be when it burdens the individual with the idea that he or she is the total master of their well-being and the direction of their life and how little this ideology contributes to possible change in the organisation of society as a whole. There are moments when rational choice is possible for the individual, and there are moments when the choices we make are irrational and sometimes damaging. Choice is a powerful mechanism in people's hands. It is the basis, after all, of any political engagement and of the political process as a whole. However, when choice is glorified as the ultimate tool by which people can shape their private lives, very little is left over for social critique. While we obsess about our individual choices, we may often fail to observe that they are hardly individual at all but are in fact highly influenced by the society in which we live.

1

WHY CHOICE MAKES US ANXIOUS

Some time ago I stopped at an upmarket grocer's in Manhattan to pick up some cheese for a dinner party. There they were: countless shelves of dairy classics, specimens of perfectly judged maturation – the soft, the blue, the hard Dutch, the crumbly English, the superior French – all with an equal claim on my attention and my purse. I was spoilt for choice.

The mechanisms of a dutiful student kicked in: I began reading the labels. If my first mistake was to enter the shop without a definite idea of the cheese I wanted, this was my second, for now the dizzying magnitude of the selection was complicated by the rhetoric on the wrappers. What made a given cheese so distinct from the hundreds of others surrounding it? Each one sang its own virtues with precision and feeling. I began to grow woozy, and not just from the smell of Camembert. Most peculiar of all was that instead of resenting the unnecessary bother that came with picking up a decent cheese – by this time I would have been grateful for 'spreadable' or 'tastes good on toast', as opposed to the 'mellifluous' and 'smoky' varieties enticing me – I was soon very angry at myself for my indecisiveness. What were the names of all those great cheeses I had tasted before? What good had all that time in France done me?

My third mistake that day was to consult the man in

charge of the cheese department. Hovering in a spotless liveried apron, his hands held primly behind his back, he appeared very knowledgeable, gladly taking on the role of authority, but still something made me suspect that perhaps his real aim was merely to offload some expensive cheeses that he would be unable to sell otherwise. Thus confusion descended into suspicion and resentment. In the end, ignoring his advice and blocking out the siren calls of the chorusing Brie and Cheddar, I decided to pick out five quite random cheeses, on the basis that they either looked great or had interesting-sounding names.

A rather bourgeois little vignette, perhaps, but one that illustrates some of the reasons why overwhelming choice can increase our anxiety and feelings of inadequacy. When Italo Calvino writes about a similar experience – that of his protagonist, Mr Palomar, visiting a Parisian Fromagerie – he conveys the overwhelming choice facing him as an existential dilemma:

> Palomar's spirit vacillates between contrasting urges: the one that aims at complete, exhaustive knowledge and could be satisfied only by tasting all the varieties; and the one that tends toward an absolute choice, the identification of the cheese that is his alone, a cheese that certainly exists even if he cannot recognize it (cannot recognize himself in it).

Overwhelmed by the museum-like experience and encyclopaedic knowledge that he discerns behind the vast array of cheese, Mr Palomar first tries to write down the names of the unknown cheeses, ones he hopes to remember for the future; but in the end, when he finally makes his choice, he chooses something rather ordinary:

> The elaborate and greedy order that he intended to make momentarily slips his mind; he stammers; he falls back on the most obvious, the most banal, the most advertised, as if the automatons of mass civilization were waiting only for this moment of uncertainty on his part in order to seize him again and have him at their mercy.[1]

For Calvino's character, imagining the story that each cheese has, the fact that 'each sort of *cheese* reveals a pasture of a different green, under a different sky', is overwhelming. His final banal choice is thus a gesture reminiscent of closing the encyclopaedia because it simply has too much information. The most advertised cheese brings solace because it takes away the uncertainty of discovering something new.

When I faced my own little ordeal at the cheese counter, I did not experience anxiety in regard to the 'different green' and 'different sky' behind each cheese, I was rather questioning my own desire in the eyes of the desire of others. First, I was bothered by the question of how others would judge the choice I made. I tried guessing what kinds of cheese my friends might like, and what unusual types of cheese I could surprise them with; and I was uneasy about the arrogant way the man behind the counter looked at me, obviously enjoying my lack of knowledge in his domain of expertise. Second, I was anxious about my perception of myself – I was angry

with myself for not being a more knowledgeable consumer. When it was all over, I was able to understand
the anxiety that my friend, a well-known law professor, admits to feeling when he's asked to choose a wine
in a restaurant. He is afraid that others will laugh at his
choice. Because of this anxiety, he usually orders very
expensive wine and, at the end of the dinner, insists on
paying for it.

When people are asked what is traumatic about
choice, they often list the following:

- they want to make an ideal choice (which is why
  they constantly switch their telephone provider, for
  example)
- they question what others will think about their
  choices, and what kind of choices others might make
  themselves
- they feel that no one is in charge in society as a whole
  (They wonder, for example, whether they really *want*
  to be in charge of selecting their electricity provider.
  They ask themselves: should this be a matter of
  individual choice?)
- they are afraid that they are not actually making a
  free choice (since they suspect that other people or
  even enterprises with their marketing strategies are
  already 'choosing' for them)

Over the past few years books and articles about
happiness have questioned why the abundance of
choice in developed capitalist societies does not bring

contentment, and why getting rich still does not make people happier.[2] Although these arguments are mostly critical of the system as it is, they nonetheless accept society's basic creed: that happiness and self-fulfilment should be our primary goals.

Yet capitalism thrives and grows with scant regard for those goals. In his novel *Happiness*™ the Canadian writer Will Ferguson plays with this idea by envisioning what would happen if people in the west ever did become truly, universally happy.[3] He describes a society where people are mesmerised by a self-help book that provides a true and easy way to fulfilment. The small book spreads like a virus. Everyone who reads it immediately abandons their old life, starts dressing more simply, stops buying make-up, does without plastic surgery, cancels their gym subscription, gives up their car and quits their job. Everywhere, office doors bear the same note: 'Gone fishing!' These newly awakened people brim with happiness – physically they become more relaxed, they smile all the time, they move gracefully and joyfully, they exude serenity. But when the masses become truly happy, capitalism is shaken to its foundations. Industries start to fall like dominoes. Deeply worried, the self-help book's publishers resolve to stop this happiness movement, on behalf of their shareholders and the world's capitalist leaders. They start searching for the book's author. Soon it is revealed that the writer is not an Indian guru, as the cover claims, but an old loner living in a trailer park. It turns out that, having been diagnosed with cancer, the man thought up the book as a way to make some money to leave to his grandson. With this aim in mind, he had simply cobbled together the main ideas contained in existing self-help manuals. The story ends when the publisher convinces the old man that his writing has done more harm than good for the progress of society. He encourages him to write a new book on how to be miserable, so that capitalism can flourish once more.

Capitalism has always played on our feelings of inadequacy, as well as on the perception that we are free to decide the path we will take in the future and thereby improve our lives. From the late seventeenth century on, the Enlightenment project promoted the idea of choice – giving rise to our modern conceptions of political freedom, the relationship between mind and body, lover and loved, child and parent. And capitalism, of course, has encouraged not only the idea of consumer choice but also the ideology of the self-made man, which allowed the individual to start seeing his own life as a series of options and possible transformations.

The idea of choice first appeared in this context in the form of an attempt to link the idea of making the most of an individual's professional life with devotion to religious ideas. In early seventeenth-century Britain there were already books offering advice on how to make the most of one's abilities and become wealthy and successful while still serving Christ and fulfilling a useful role in the community.[4] The term 'self-made man', however, is usually credited to Henry Clay, a self-made man himself and one of America's leading early industrialists. (Ironically, Clay was also a proponent of the so-called 'American System', the plan for a command economy in which, his critics argued, individual workers were reduced to the level of trained apes.) Benjamin Franklin also cherished the idea of the self-made man: he stressed that the most successful men in history were of humble origins and were often self-taught. These men were marked by an ability to rise above the difficulties of life, to seize every opportunity in the pursuit of some honest and worthy aim. Underlying the ideal of the self-made man was the conviction that getting rich was the natural result of a man realising his particular talents. 'No man could do justice to the genius within him,' Emerson wrote, 'without demanding more of the world than a bare subsistence.'[5]

The eighteenth-century American dream of the self-made man underpinned the famous rags-to-riches stories of Horatio Alger in the second half of the nineteenth century, in which bootblacks, pedlars, buskers and others from the ranks of the impoverished rise to middle-class respectability. Here to be 'self-made' means to have climbed the ladder of success. Above all, the self-made man is independent from social constraints. With sheer determination and hard work, he could rise above the social and economic conditions into which he was born. He confronts the world with an all-conquering will, and obstacles only help to shape him. By confronting and dealing with adversity in a heroic fashion, a man can become a true conqueror, of himself and of the world.

A long-standing debate, unresolved to the present day, about what the state owes its citizens and what those citizens owe one another, peaked in the nineteenth century. The question was whether an individual was obliged to consider the welfare of all or whether his ambition should be given free rein. While critics of the 'laissez-faire' approach insisted on regulatory legislation and the active intervention of the state in economic affairs, defenders of free trade clung to the belief that good intentions, personal rectitude and the universal laws of moral retribution afforded sufficient protection. Some books on self-help from the end of the nineteenth century which still had a strongly religious tone pointed out that a self-made man needed extra moral reserves and that his success was the proof that he had found and used them. Such books also stressed the businessman's responsibility for the welfare of his fellows and rejected the view that one man's outstanding success probably meant the failure of many others. Optimists thus saw every triumph as opening the way for more triumphs, as long as you were honest in your dealings.

Christian self-help books which took a Calvinistic line, however, tried to reconcile readers to their lot in life: just as there were limited places in heaven, so it was impossible for everyone to enjoy worldly success. There were winners and losers, but in truth men were not fighting one another; they were in a constant struggle with their own lower selves.

At the turn of the twentieth century, however, the tone of many self-help guides to business slowly changed. The notion of picking off competitors and claiming scalps gradually gained acceptance. When a man tried to succeed in life, he was embarking not only on a struggle with his inner self or with the circumstances that he was born into; he also needed to focus on overtaking others who were in pursuit of their own success. Choosing the direction of one's life was thus linked to the post-Darwinian idea of the survival of the fittest, and life was perceived as a kind of battlefield where only the strongest or the most cunning succeeded. As the century continued, the entry of women into the workforce further modified the idea of the self-made man. Could there be 'self-made' women? And if there could, what was so manly any more about being self-made?

Nowadays, becoming 'self-made' is not so straightforward. In the developed world a young man or woman does not simply follow a steady path up the social and economic ladder: survival, even relative prosperity, may be taken for granted. So the mission becomes *self-invention*. For postmodern professionals life itself is a kind of artwork or enterprise, something to be refined, revised, improved on, and success consists of its fullest possible expression. The idea of choice has thus become radicalised: everything in life has become a matter of decisions that need to be made carefully in order to come close to the ideal of happiness and self-fulfilment that society promotes.

My life, my corporation

The times we live in are dominated by impatient capital. There is a constant desire for rapid returns. But it is not only corporations and financial services that are pressured to manage every risk and to maximise returns. We are all encouraged to act like corporations: to make a life-plan of goals, make long-term investments, be flexible, restructure our life's enterprise and take the risks necessary in order to increase profits.

An internet entrepreneur who built a huge company during the dot-com bubble once told me a story of how difficult it was, after the bubble burst, to sack his enthusiastic young workers. He remembered one conversation as particularly agonising. When he broke the bad news, the young man looked for a moment as though he was going to burst into tears. But then he quickly composed himself, took out a notebook and asked exactly what he had done wrong, what areas he might not have worked hard enough in and, especially, how he might do better in his next job. Moved by the intensity of this young man's reaction, the boss insisted there was nothing wrong with his performance; the market had simply forced the company to downsize. But the young man insisted; he needed more feedback. He wanted to 'work on himself' and become an even better employee next time around.

Not long ago a person who had been fired would be more likely to blame external circumstances, but we now are compelled to evaluate ourselves and work out why it was that we failed to keep the job. Evaluation is the ultimate buzzword of today's employment culture. In British universities teachers spend half their time writing reports on students, programmes or academic colleagues. In international corporations around the world employees are not only evaluated by their bosses but are asked to evaluate themselves. The constant process of evaluation and monitoring which is crucial to industrial manufacture has become internalised as a way of controlling our behaviour. Since the 'accuracy' of one's own evaluation is then measured against that of a manager or superior, this in itself produces a good measure of anxiety.

The more isolated we become from a real engagement with the social and political sphere, the more we are propelled toward self-mastery. The less predictable and controllable the course of our life becomes, the more we are urged to chart our own course, to 'master' our destiny and to remodel ourselves. In addition to the actual hours spent on the job, which have increased dramatically, we are supposed to engage in retraining and re-schooling for new types of work, to stay looking young and healthy and to stay searching for what our 'true calling' may actually be.

To live a successful life now is to become a successful investor. We not only need to learn the logic of the stock market and become our own financial advisor; we are also urged to see our own lives as an investment. The platitude of 'investing' time and care in a relationship has been around a long time, but now we are told that the time and love we give our children are also a literal investment. Quality parenting time will supposedly produce a satisfactory child: one that will reflect well on us, fulfil our own unfulfilled dreams and aspirations and support us financially in our old age. Only from this viewpoint do such time and care, necessarily subtracted from work, seem usefully spent. With spouses and friends too we invest our energy so that down the line we may draw on the emotional reserves that such relationships create. Willard F. Harley, a famous American marriage counsellor, has mapped out precisely how such emotional reserves should work in order to yield optimal companionship.

Imagine a couple in which the husband loves football and the wife loves going on long walks with her husband. The intelligent couple will put savings into this emotional nest egg during times when the relationship is solid. The wife, for example, will go with her husband to watch football, even though she hates it, and the husband will join her on walks, although he would rather be in front of the television. In times of crisis one partner may start withdrawing affection; he or she may get angry and stop joining the other in activities they used to share. The reserves in the love bank then slowly become depleted, to the point of either emptying or even going into the red. When such a crisis arises, the marriage counsellor suggests that a couple needs to search for the help of an adviser such as him, who will help them to restructure their emotional investments banks and rebuild their funds.

No one can deny that marriages work better if the partners spend time together, and that sometimes this requires compromise on shared activities. But today's advice culture seeks to depict love and the emotions as elements of life that we can rationally master, even though this is the domain where unconscious impulses and feelings are at their most powerful. There is thus a desire now to master these unconscious impulses, to find a way to alter uncomfortable feelings as well as to control the nature of attraction. With the ever dominant idea that life outcomes are simply a matter of choice and that it is up to us to decide how we want to live, love and sexuality are made to seem as easily manageable as, say, a career or choosing a holiday. Popular magazines and newspapers give the impression that we should be able to have the most fantastic, imaginative sex possible and that there are endless new ways to increase our sexual satisfaction. Our own sex lives seem flatly ordinary when compared with the prevailing ideas of what sex should look, sound and feel like, according to the media. If in Victorian times sex was taboo, nowadays it is almost as though *not* having sex is taboo, and people keep quiet about their own sex lives while imagining that everyone else has the kind of sex life depicted in the magazines or on television. This belief increases our feelings of inadequacy, while at the same time fuelling the desire on which a vast industry thrives.

The ideology of choice has now so deeply penetrated our ideas about the nature of sexual satisfaction that, when our love life fails to meet the cultural ideals of eternal erotic bliss and endless play with new techniques, we are supposed to do something about it – to spend money and time to make it better. The mock documentary *Unscrewed* gives an example of such a consumerist approach to sexuality.[6] The film follows a young couple who are having sexual problems. Frustrated that

their otherwise loving relationship is not sexually fulfilling, they decide to do everything possible to find the
missing spark. First they consult a urologist, who checks
their physical ability to have sex and, after an unpleasant
series of tests, gives them various drugs and creams to
remedy the problem. Next the couple turn to a tantric
teacher, who provides them with relaxation techniques
and suggests how they can get in touch with their sexual
inner selves. Third, they decide to try a sex therapist,
who is not just interested in talking through the couple's
thoughts about sex but also wants to see how they physically approach sex. On an impromptu bed the couple are
encouraged to demonstrate how they usually position
themselves when they start making love. The therapist
immediately concludes that the starting position, with
the man above the woman, is far too domineering for
her. The couple are then advised to change their behaviour in the bedroom and are also encouraged to take a
weekend break to try sex in different surroundings. Surprisingly, this idea works, and during the trip the couple
are finally able to have sex. However, when they return
home they decide to separate. The film nicely shows how
a person may make a rational decision to achieve a goal
while at the same time unconsciously doing everything
possible to avoid it. It may be that what held this couple
together was the very lack of sexual satisfaction or the
mutual search for a solution, while the realisation of their
quest proved unsatisfactory.

Guilty at what we may feel is our comparative lack
of sexual satisfaction, we try to find ways to manipulate

our own and our partner's desire in order to improve our sex life. At the same time, we also try to find ways of 'doing something' about our emotions. The idea of choice has deeply penetrated our perception of feelings, as though we can 'choose' whether or not to have them. Painful emotions, in particular, we try to get rid of. A subject search on Amazon.com for 'anger' results in tens of thousands of hits for books dealing with this issue. A quick look at the bestselling titles gives the impression that anger is a huge problem in today's society: countless books offer to teach you how to get rid of it. *Anger Management*, *Overcoming Anger*, *Beyond Anger*, *Conquering Anger*, *Letting Go of Anger*, *Anger Control*, *Healing Anger*, *Working with Anger* and *Taking Charge of Anger* are just some of the titles supposed to help us deal with this renegade emotion. The next step is to *Honour your Anger*, to go *From Anger to Forgiveness* and, especially, to realise that *Anger is a Choice*. Introducing the idea of choice into the area of emotions, however, only serves to increase feelings of anxiety and guilt. No matter how much we may try to manipulate our feelings of anger with the techniques these books suggest, in the end we will probably only feel angry at ourselves for not overcoming this painful emotion. But although anger appears to be something that we need to control or get rid of, we should not forget that it is a necessary feeling, one that precipitates social change. Attempts to rid people of anger can be thus taken as another way of pacifying them and directing their attention away from social problems and towards individual ones.

Self-help

The perception that the direction of one's life, as well as one's emotions, is something one can choose has contributed to a vast self-help industry. Between 1972 and 2000 there was a huge increase in the number of self-help books published in the USA. During that period somewhere between 33 and 50 per cent of Americans purchased a self-help book. The industry accelerated particularly towards the end of the twentieth century, and in the five-year period between 1991 and 1996 the American booksellers' report showed that there was almost a 100 per cent increase in self-help publications.[7] Noticing that the people around him were looking to change their own lives by reading a book written by someone else, George Carlin noted: 'That's not self-help, that's help.'

Generally speaking, self-help books are designed to alleviate our anxiety about our own well-being, our standing in society at large, and to suggest ways to improve our lifes. However, they tend to offer widely varying explanations and solutions for people's troubles. Some reflect a deep religious belief and thus, for example, advise people to succumb to a higher power when faced with adversity, and to accept everything as it is; others suggest that the world exists only in the form in which we perceive it, and therefore everything can be changed with the right kind of thinking. There are books that describe the mind as a computer, a mechanism that just needs to be programmed with the right feelings and behavioural patterns. Others believe that all success is linked to the creative powers of the universe. Shakti Gawain, for example, explains that material success happens when 'you learn how to listen to the universe and act on it, [and] then money increasingly comes into your life. It flows in an easy, effortless, and joyful way because there is no sacrifice involved.'[8]

In the 1970s, when the world faced numerous oil crises, self-help took an interesting turn. Many of the books started promoting the idea of survival, a turn to personal power and the need to look after Number One. They began describing life as a battlefield, as a game in which one needs to play 'tough', as a journey through a jungle.[9] The reader was addressed as a combatant, a contestant, an explorer or a traveller in search of a great reward (often attained only by eliminating others). The reward was either material or spiritual success. The idea that life is an assault course, a rat race or a poker game and that only the strongest survive was linked to the empowering message that we should not regard ourselves as victims.

In discussions about the nature of victimhood the idea of choice has led to the idea that one can choose to be a victim or a survivor and that individuals can choose how they regard their suffering and can decide what to do about it. The mantra in scores of self-help books that only we can control ourselves and that we have a choice as to how we regard negative events and circumstances has become linked to the ideology of positive thinking, which often gives step-by-step prescriptions for how to overcome set-backs in one's life. While some self-help theories promote positive action and behaviour, others promote positive thinking. The first kind often foster unreal expectations about what people can actually do, and the second raise false hopes about the power of thinking. These theories play on the idea of the individual's omnipotence in a particular way. On the one hand, there is the idea of all-powerful individuals who with their sheer determination can change the world around them and thus increase their own well-being. On the other, there is a rejection of reality as such and a perception that individuals have power over the way they see reality around them and that by seeing things differently you can even change them.

In these times of crisis and uncertainty the ideology of positive thinking plays an essential role in masking the need to rethink the nature of social inequalities and trying to find alternatives to the way capitalism has been developing. When individuals are made to feel they are the masters of their own destiny, and when positive thinking is offered as the panacea for the ills that they suffer as the result of social injustice, social critique is increasingly replaced by self-critique.

The crucial point about self-help guides is that they manifestly do not work. Despite a huge and hungry readership, they have failed to create a happier and mentally healthier society. And therein lies their real achievement: rather than curing unhappiness, these books have strengthened the idea that misery is everywhere. They have drawn attention to the countless flaws and inadequacies in the average person and kept us busy with our own failings. So we seek out ever more self-help. More importantly, the genre is one of countless subliminal mechanisms that prod the sore spots in the collective and individual psyche. Reminders of the ways in which we could be better keep us feeling inadequate, keep us trying to be better and work harder. 'Self-help' relies on people failing to meet the expectations they create and thus needing more help, more books and more coaching.

In other words, 'self-help' increases the very sense of inadequacy and paranoia that it supposedly seeks to alleviate. It is a self-sustaining market. As far as wider societal goals are concerned, it is successful in creating, rather than dispelling, guilt and anxiety, as the story of Jennifer Niesslein mentioned in the Introduction illustrates. If life is a battlefield, then one must be forever at war; and if positive thoughts alter life for the better, we must be vigilant against any negative ones; and if everything depends on the individual, then we can blame no one else when the course of treatment fails.

Coaching

The paradox of the promotion of choice as the ultimate idea of post-industrial capitalism lies in the fact that it has opened the way for all kinds of new services intended to offer ways of dealing with the overwhelming choice we are now faced with and restricting our ever-expanding desires. Choice involves the freedom of the individual to determine the direction of their life, but paradoxically the latter is often quick to give up on this freedom and search for an authority to help deal with all the options as long as they have the power to choose which authority to consult. The proliferation of various kinds of coaches whom we can temporarily defer to is a response to this demand. Yet while the coach is someone we can turn to and ask which direction to take, it is important that he or she does not appear to be or behave like an authority who demands to be obeyed but is more of a benevolent helper whom the individual has chosen to listen to.

The term 'coach' used only to mean someone in charge of an athletics or sports team, but in the last decade it has also come to mean someone who can direct a person's life the way a football coach organises his team's defence. In sport, the coach (as distinct from a 'trainer') is in charge of overseeing every level of one's athletic performance. He or she is a mixture of parent, friend, therapist and cheerleader. For the relationship between coach and player to work, the player must have complete trust in the coach's ability to judge his abilities in any context. The coach is thus a master whom the player freely chooses to follow. In modern life we look to the coach as someone who will increase our power to succeed or who will restore it in times of self-doubt or when we feel ourselves to be faltering.[10]

From the coach's perspective, the main goal is to motivate. The coach responds to the diffused anxiety that is part of contemporary life. But the whole ideology of life-coaching insists that existential crisis and anxiety represent just a plain lack of willpower or a crisis of confidence. The coach does not ask what is causing anxiety in her student's professional environment, for example, but focuses on how the student can change his behaviour.[11] The ultimate goal of coaching is to reintegrate the student into the traditional roles of production and consumption. As a new form of social control, coaching encourages individuals to become more and more self-regulating, to adapt constantly to the changes in society around them. Whoever is capable of total self-control, of fully determining his desire, will fulfil his potential and realise his goals. Under the coach's instruction the student learns that life can be mastered. But the irony is that this mastery comes only when he submits to the coach and learns from the coach how to conform to his environment.

My house – myself

As we work to improve ourselves and our lives, so we need also to create around us the environment best suited to our ideal existence. Since we are increasingly powerless in terms of our ability to change the society we live in, we try to change our immediate environment – our home. The latter may long have been understood as an extension of the self: it is now also an essential part of one's personal development. The house is almost a living thing, something that acquires a certain power over the human subject. Our home is perceived as a prosthesis of ourselves, with the hidden potential to influence our creative self. The house is simultaneously the mirror of the self and its incubator. 'You are your home', is the sort of remark one might overhear. 'Your inner self will find fulfilment as long as you create the right environment for it' might be another point of view on people's relationship to their home. These two rather contradictory views both seem appropriate in the context of today's ideology of the private space.

The 'Your house – yourself' mantra, however, leaves us with the tremendous burden of choosing from all the various furnishings, styles and accessories available today. The practice of Feng Shui, like other forms of coaching, offers a way to relieve the 'tyranny of choice' in domestic affairs and delegate it to others.

Feng Shui, which literally means 'wind and water', is an ancient Chinese art of interior design that seeks to place the individual in harmony with his or her environment. By placing, decorating and furnishing correctly, one's personal 'chi' increases, thus improving health and increasing growth in relationships and opportunities for wealth, health and success. 'Applying some Feng Shui concepts to your own home', one Feng Shui website suggests, 'may be exactly what's needed to replace an empty void in your life. As you study the art of Feng Shui, you will change the way you look at your home and by changing the quality of your home you are simultaneously improving your quality of life.'[12] This ancient soft science thus allows us to fine-tune our destinies by adjusting our furniture. According to the wisdom of Feng Shui, if I want to get rich, I should place fake money or a bowl of foreign coins in my room. However, I must be careful not to have a toilet in the area that contributes to prosperity, as money can easily be poured down the drain. One solution is offered: keep the toilet lid closed. I must even monitor what kinds of images I place on the wall. Another Feng Shui site says: 'Avoid placing photographs of yourself when you were going through a "broke phase" (such as when you were a student in college or just recently divorced) here. You might repeat the situation!' [13]

The idea that streamlining and de-cluttering provide a direct path to prosperity has been catching on in other forms in the developed world lately. In the USA, one can hire a consultant who will make an inventory of your life and 'simplify' it, for a substantial fee. As a teaser, we get the following advice:

> For every single item in your home, whether it's the antique clock on the mantel (that's been broken since 1974) or the shiny new bread machine your mother gave you for Christmas, you **MUST** ask yourself:
>
> - Does this one object make me happy?
> - Do I love my home *more* because of it?
> - Does it have a place in the life of my dreams?
>
> If so, Green Light – it stays. If not – PITCH IT! Throw it out, donate it to a worthy cause, or have a good old-fashioned yard sale.

Why is it so important to de-clutter? The author here gives the following explanation for free (and, of course, a more elaborate one for a charge):

———

I once consulted for a woman who became unbearably depressed whenever she spent much time in her home. As we sat in her living room together, I asked her to look at each piece of furniture, each trinket she owned, and ask herself how she felt about it. It turns out that she was miserable because of a beautiful, and very expensive, vase that stood in the corner. The vase had come to her as a result of a nasty divorce, and because of its monetary value, she felt like she should hold on to it. But the memories associated with it had turned it into a black hole, draining her energy every time she was in the same room with it. Take a walk around your own home this evening, and pay attention to your energy levels – I guarantee you'll be shocked at some of the emotions you'll find tied up in your stuff.

If we are sad or depressed, then, we should search among the furniture for the solution. Perhaps not surprisingly, our obsession with doing up our homes surges during a recession. In times of economic crisis people turn even more to television advice on how to redecorate cheaply, how to make one's house more attractive to potential buyers and how to spice up one's life by making changes to one's flat – even if it is simply by adding a fresh coat of paint.

Choice and denial

The ideology that promotes choice so forcefully paradoxically requires some form of denial, which psychoanalysis sees as an essential mechanism through which

---

the individual deals with his or her inner conflicts. With consumers, the first level of denial is linked to the view that there are no limits to consumption and that anyone can pursue it, but the second level of denial involves the need to deny the actual quantity of consumption, to perceive consumption as something that has not actually happened. The unrestrained consumer thus creates the illusion that their consumption does not involve painful consequences – i.e. that the debt does not need to be repaid.

The consumer who is going through circles of consumption and de-cluttering and who constantly seems to be failing in the self-mastery that is promoted by the ideology of choice can often be plagued by doubt, and the abundance of options easily leads to regret, which is why denial may help him or her to avoid these feelings. It's interesting to note, in this context, the different ways in which customers offer their credit cards to the person at the till. Wealthy buyers will toss their card nonchalantly onto the counter, demonstrating how trivial the expense is, how unworthy of hesitation. A more careful customer in a similar situation will pause. When she hands over her card, it looks as though, for a brief moment, she may take it back – as though, at the same time, she is offering and not offering her card to the cashier. She is grappling with the knowledge, however inchoate, that she will one day have to pay that debt. And yet most of the time she will surrender the card and shake off her worries.

This reluctance to confront debt was the basis of our consumption in the decades leading up to the financial crisis. Buy now, pay later. And while consumers learned to shuffle their credit cards and put off the final reckoning, the big financial institutions promoted the fantasy that payback time would never come on a large scale. During those years, when consumers were encouraged only to pay interest on their debts, a way of thinking developed that the French psychoanalyst Octave Mannoni called 'I know very well, but …'. It's a self-delusion similar to the one that allows children to continue fantasising about Santa Claus well past the point when they rationally know he doesn't exist. Consumers know that they have debts, but unconsciously act to preserve the illusion that everything will be OK, that somehow the debts will be paid off.

This wilful forgetfulness about money is similar to the way many people cope with the idea of death. Reporting on the effects of the economic collapse, *The New York Times* investigated high rates of depression in retirement communities where people were facing huge losses to their pension funds. In these communities there was an atmosphere of bereavement. People behaved as though someone had died. The psychotherapist Barbara Goldsmith, who helps mourners such as these, says they are indeed dealing with death: 'their money died.'

How are we to understand this overlap between death and economic loss? Often we save money in order to cheat death, or to live on through the inheritance we leave to our children. (To keep the conversation about money going, we write wills that keep them tied to us.) Money is perceived as a security blanket against decay

– as protection against illness, infirmity, solitude. But at the same time we derive a special enjoyment from spending it freely, in defying death. That is why money in psychoanalytic terms is often perceived in an anal way – as sublime shit that both fascinates us and horrifies us. How else can we understand the great pleasure that comes from throwing money away – from gambling or buying things we don't need?

American psychologists looking at the behaviour of middle-class people who frequent Las Vegas casinos found high rates of depression. Most of the gamblers knew, rationally, that the casinos always win in the end, and in looking back at their own experience they realised that they lost most of the time. Many gamblers worked long hours to earn their living, often at the expense of spending time with family or pursuing hobbies. They were frugal when it came to purchases and were willing to drive long distances to discount stores in order to save a couple of dollars. In Las Vegas, however, they threw money into the machines without hesitation. But at the end of the day they resumed their frugal habits, forming long queues to save money at the all-you-can-eat buffet. Such games with money, which go from saving to purging, show the uncanny character that we attribute to it: money is obviously not a living thing, but the way we kill it again and again shows how uncertain we are about its power. It is as though throwing it away alleviates the anxiety that it provokes. Yet the feeling of guilt quickly kicks in, which is why we start obsessively saving again.

Businesses perform the same unaccountable dance

of caution and risk. Once I was invited to give a talk to the CEO's meeting of a large corporation. The organisers advised me that my talk should be upbeat, since participants do not like to listen to anything negative. When I listened to other speakers at the meeting, I felt like a member of a religious cult. The CEOs were shown a chart about their future earnings on which all the signs were pointing upwards: *the future will be fantastic*. Psychologists gave lectures about the personality traits of great leaders and here too each trait translated into an avenue to increased profits. The audience sat in a trance, then applauded at the end of each talk like fans in a football stadium. Denial was omnipresent. Leaders of the corporation were avoiding anything that might shatter the pervasive mood of optimism. The participants basked in self-congratulatory feelings of success and appeared to have no doubt that the future would bring increased profits and success in overtaking competitors.

Clearly our generation has thrived on the illusion of progress, while privately the idea of ever-expanding possibility has only made us more anxious. The more we have tried to convince ourselves that choice brings greater satisfaction, the less we have actually seemed to enjoy having it.

Anxiety and choice

Philosophers have long observed a connection between anxiety and choice. For Kierkegaard, anxiety grew

---

directly out of freedom – out of the need to face the possibility of possibility. Sartre glossed this by saying that a person standing in front of the abyss is anxious not because he may fall, but because he is free to throw himself over the edge.

Although we may feel overwhelmed by consumer choice and the pressure to turn our life into an art project or a well-run enterprise, we should remember that the problem today is not that choices are available to us in the developed world. Rather, the problem is that the idea of rational choice, transferred from the domain of economics, has been glorified as the only kind of choice we have.

There have been a number of critiques of the idea of choice that penetrates today's consumer society. Barry Schwartz, for example, in his book *The Paradox of Choice: Why More is Less,* gives many examples from psychological research which show that people exposed to less choice are more satisfied.[14] In order to limit the dissatisfaction that overwhelming consumer choices bring, Schwartz proposes various forms of self-restraint. He argues that we should 'choose when to choose', be a chooser not a picker, be content with 'good enough', make our decisions non-reversible, cultivate an attitude of gratitude, regret less, anticipate adaptation, control our expectations, refrain from making social comparisons, and, especially, 'learn to love constraints'.

In a paradoxical way the idea of choice is already actually bound up with these recommendations for self-restraint. All the advice on how to 'de-clutter' our lives and bodies is based on the idea that we need to be more organised, more efficient, more in control. Self-restraint is a key idea also in books that offer advice on how to live a healthy life and especially in the ever-growing dieting industry. Popular books with titles such as *How the Rich Get Thin* describe how women from posh New York neighbourhoods (with whom an average American girl is supposed to identify) apparently plan everything in their lives to perfection and are very much in control of every aspect of their life. The problem, however, is that women who are trying to fashion an ideal body and an ideal life are continuously made to feel that they could do even better and are thus creating ever new prohibitions for themselves.

The ideology of choice appears to be liberating, since it relies on the idea of multiple possibilities. If at times of abundance of choice the old limitations ceased to exist, new self-prohibitions quickly took their place. Such changes in the nature of prohibition have already occurred in the past. After the sexual revolution, for example, new celibacy movements began emerging, along with dating rules that urged women to make themselves less available sexually and thus increase men's desire.

The paradox, however, is that, although people often invent new self-prohibitions, one cannot invent them as a *rational* proposal of new forms of self-binding, as suggested by Barry Schwartz. Psychoanalysis has shown us that people do not usually act directly and deliberately to maximise their pleasure and minimise their pain. Often enough, they know, rationally, that something is damaging, but either they can't stop or they find some kind of satisfaction in the pain. Some people may rationally claim that they want more happiness in their lives, but at an unconscious level they seem much more attracted by the opposite.

Even if choice appears to be such an individual matter, the way people make choices is essentially linked to the way they forge relationships with others and how they think others see them. Thus it is not so much that people invent forms of self-restraint off their own back as that their choices are very much bound by what they perceive society values as the right choice. This explains why, paradoxically, the new self-made individual models him- or herself on celebrity culture: on the one hand addressed as an individual, totally free to create an identity from scratch, but on the other following an arbitrary popular model of who to be, often derived from the life of a celebrity. This reflects a major change in the way that the individual identifies with social ideals under late capitalism, a shift that has also occurred in the way people today identify with authorities chosen and self- imposed and how they perceive themselves within society as a whole.

CHOOSING THROUGH OTHERS' EYES

In Western society we can choose our identity, our sexual orientation and our religion. We can choose whether or not to have children. We can remodel our bodies and even change gender. But once we've surrendered ourselves to all these contingencies, what is left to dictate our choices? Who do we become when everything about us is optional?

In a debate with graduate law students about the choice of identity, one student who stridently insisted that in postmodern times he feels totally free to play with many identities even linked his obedience of rules to different choices that he makes every day with regard to his identity. How he obeys social prohibitions depends, for example, on which identity he is temporarily taking on. In the morning, on his way to the law office where he works, he obeys the sign at the edge of a park that says, 'Do not trespass'. In the afternoon, when he's wearing jeans and free from job obligations, he's less inclined to obey. And in the evening, in his free time, he feels free to take on many different identities on the internet: he participates in a Muslim forum pretending to be a Muslim; sometimes he frequents gay internet sites pretending that he is gay; occasionally he presents himself as a woman or a foreigner.

The same fluidity is available when it comes to national

identity. When I first met Annu, a young anthropologist who studied in Britain, I knew that she had been born in India but I also heard that her family was of French origin. Then I met her parents. Both looked distinctly Indian. Her mother was tall and dark-skinned, with long black hair, and she was wearing a sari. On her forehead was the tilaka or red dot signifying that she was a married Hindu woman. Her father was dark-haired and could easily pass as Indian too. Both parents spoke English with a Hindi accent. Since they had just arrived from Calcutta, where they lived, I concluded that they must both be Indians, and perhaps they had spent some time in France earlier in their lives. It was a great surprise to learn from Annu that they were Indian by choice. Born and raised in France, they decided in the 1970s that they had had enough of Western life, and they moved to India. There they embraced Indian culture and the Indian way of life, to the point of dressing in traditional Indian clothes, speaking Hindi and raising their children as Indian families did. They had escaped Western capitalism, with its emphasis on the idea of choice, but they had also taken it with them. Their assimilation into Indian society was not the matter of economic necessity that it is for most immigrants; it was simply a matter of choosing a lifestyle that appealed to them.

Although one's choice of identity may look at first like a totally autonomous act of self-creation, usually it depends on many other factors. Several years ago in 2004, a winner of one of the *Big Brother* television series in the UK, Nadia Almada, revealed herself to be a transgendered woman. When she learned that she had won, her response was 'Now I am recognised as a woman.' What the British TV audience found seductive about her was that she had accomplished her dream of making something completely different of herself. With her self-transformation, she embodied the very idea of self-creation. However, the fact that she had entered a form of television competition and her delight in achieving public recognition as a woman, also demonstrated how much we need other people to bolster our freely made choices, to define who we are.

Choice and other people

The British psychoanalyst Darian Leader observed in his book *Why Do Women Write More Letters Than They Post?* that when women go shopping they usually want to buy a dress that no other woman will have, while men usually do the opposite and try to buy the same clothes as everyone else.[1] The same double-bind now afflicts both sexes in the developed world. Men and women are told they should make something unique of themselves, but at the same time they are given detailed prescriptions about how this unique individual should look, what career he or she should have and, especially, which celebrity he or she should resemble.

The television show *I Want a Famous Face* follows people who decide to get plastic surgery on their faces to make them look more like their favourite celebrity.[2]

In a slightly less dramatic format, *Extreme Makeover* presents plastic surgery as the ultimate path to a better life and follows those taking part at every stage of their glorious self-transformation. After going through the makeover, they often look like someone else. They don't just want to look different; they want others to see them differently. In one episode, for example, a woman called Melissa decides she wants to look different for her tenth high school reunion. After being teased at school for her looks, she now wants to take her revenge.[3] For her, a new body has thus become the solution to the trauma and resentment of being an outcast teenager. Psychoanalysts now hear similar demands for quick, dramatic change every day, with people saying 'I want to re-invent myself'. In psychoanalysis, of course, the purpose is not to answer a patient's demands for change but to help them understand what lies behind the desire. Cosmetic surgery, however, has stepped in to answer the patient's call; it has become the all-powerful science, promising instant and all-encompassing change.

Just as a person can feel that they don't inhabit the appropriate body to express their identity and thus constantly search for body transformation, so a person can feel inadequate with other identities taken on in life. The overarching problem with crafting an identity is that a person may temporarily find solace in saying, for example, that he is a teacher, a father, a husband or a musician. But none of these identities says everything there is to say about who he actually is. No matter how much an individual tries to 'become himself', he will necessarily fail, because there will always be something within him that cannot easily be defined by an external identity. The ego (one's self-perception) is a very shaky structure, easily undermined by unconscious drives and desires. It is possible to repress those drives for a while and feel like a capable, rational subject, but eventually they will reveal themselves in the form of idiosyncratic behaviour, slips of the tongue, even illnesses. The perception that one can craft an identity by copying that of someone else has created particular problems in today's society.

The cult of celebrity

The message that anyone can achieve a life of glamour and celebrity, if they choose it and apply themselves, has led countless people to abandon essential elements of their lives in the pursuit of an unattainable fantasy. After the fantastic success of the Russian tennis players Anna Kournikova and Maria Sharapova, for example, tennis courts began popping up in remote villages all across Russia. Poor Russian parents latched on to the dream that their little girl could become a champion, a star and a role model. Many of them made enormous sacrifices in terms of both time and money – sometimes to the point of selling all their possessions – to support their child's intensive training.[4] And yet the chances that anyone can become a tennis star, no matter how hard they train, are minuscule. American research estimates that in the

USA only 1 child in 10,000 gets an athletic scholarship to college[5] and only 6 out of 10,000 get the chance to become professional athletes.[6] Even if one were to tell these Russian parents that the chances of their daughter becoming a new Sharapova are minimal, most would not be persuaded to give up. When Serena Williams won her first US Open in 1999, she said: 'It was my father's dream and now it is mine.' It is often revealed, after a young tennis player reaches the top, that the dream of stardom was not originally theirs but came from their parents. Sports and entertainment marketing constantly drives home the idea that everyone should try to become a star, to rise above their social constraints. But in many cases the dream is twice removed from individual choice: first, it begins not with the player but with their parents; and second, the ambition is modelled on an already established career – that of Maria Sharapova, for example, in the case of young women Russian tennis players.

It may be hard for us to accept that what we think of as pure individual choice is so often contingent on the perceptions and influences of others. We want to believe we are in total control and entirely autonomous. And yet we are nagged by the sense that we don't know enough, or that we're not properly equipped, to make an informed choice. Then, when we hear from an authority, we question the value of that input.

In his book, *Fame Junkies: The Hidden Truths behind America's Favorite Addiction*, Jake Halpern looks at the way celebrities' personal assistants develop identities that are powerfully, often disturbingly, influenced by their bosses.[7] In the early stages of the job assistants live their whole lives through their famous employer and gradually start losing their identity as a separate person. The first crisis comes when the PA has to consider spending some time away from the boss. A sense of loss emerges, and horror at being a nobody. Sooner or later the PA realises that no one actually knows her name. When she leaves the job, she has to wean herself off the powerful presence of their boss. On the one hand, she feels that she has lost her status as an extension of a celebrity, but on the other hand, she sees for the first time how much of her normal life she has sacrificed while working. Old friends have been dropped, family members alienated and other possibilities for the future lost sight of.

The demands on a celebrity's PA are similar to those placed on a member of a cult. As Halpern points out: 'With both celebrities and cults the attendants feel important – helping the great ones to function they are also so close to power that they can almost see it and touch it – that is intoxicating.'[8] But the price is high: cult leaders and celebrities are greedy institutions. Halpern thus concludes: 'We wear clothing decorated with their name, we buy all their products, we travel where they go, we talk about them incessantly, and the most we get is a slight buzz from being in their outermost orbits.'[9]

Identifying with people we set up as role models, however, is never a simple matter and may reflect our attitudes to more traditional authority figures, such as parents. While we may love and respect them on one level, we may also find fault with them, especially as we get older. So too with celebrities, whom we put on a pedestal before enjoying cutting them down to size and exposing them as ordinary people – just like us. The popular magazine *US Weekly* tries hard to present celebrities as friendly, down-to-earth, neighbourly people. The title of one of their sections is 'Stars – They're Just Like Us!' 'Our readers feel like Jennifer Aniston is their best friend', the magazine's editor has said; 'Jen became everyone's best friend in the TV show *Friends*, and then she breaks up with Brad and has this big trauma.' Has this raised magazine sales? 'Absolutely!' [10] By using a diminutive form of the star's first name (Jen) the magazine creates the impression that there is no distinction between her and us, that celebrities are just normal people with the same problems as everyone else. Such (false) intimacy makes it easy to draw the conclusion that everyone can become a celebrity, given the necessary media exposure. Becoming a celebrity is thus a choice available to us all.

The desire to identify with celebrities can also be understood in a slightly more complex way by introducing the concept of 'interpassivity' coined by the Austrian philosopher Robert Phaller. [11] Interpassivity occurs between an individual and his or her proxy, who is charged with experiencing something on the other's behalf. In Serbia people hire women to cry at funerals, for example, to mourn on their behalf; Buddhists have praying mills praying for them; and by the same token, people record films they will never watch, because the recording equipment is in a way watching the film for them.

———

When it comes to celebrities, some people act outrageously in imitation of those they identify with, while for others the celebrity takes on a proxy role, behaving outrageously so the fan does not have to and can enjoy the vicarious thrill of the celebrity's excesses without having to take on any of the risks involved. To identify with a celebrity, then, is often not to copy them but rather to assume a kind of distance. A young girl might very well copy what Paris Hilton is wearing while shunning Hilton's lifestyle: Paris Hilton is a proxy who lives a wild, glamorous and damaging life so that the young girl doesn't have to.

Identification, however, does not mean simply looking like someone else: it is also concerned with the formation of an ideal self. We attach ourselves to an ideal, and then must suffer the trauma of failing to live up to it. Researchers Lori Neighbors and Jeffrey Sob followed the dieting patterns of 272 engaged women who were, on average, six months from their wedding day. Seventy per cent were trying to lose more than 20lb., and another 20 per cent were closely tracking their weight to ensure that they didn't gain. 'People take their bodies on as projects', the researchers wrote. 'And one of the times you want that project to be the most successful is on your wedding day.' [12] The brides were skipping meals, going on liquid diets, fasting, taking laxatives or unprescribed diet pills and supplements. Even if they were going to have to continue suffering the same agonies or else put all the weight back on after the big day, they were determined to make their wedding day itself a moment of pure perfection.

The image of a perfect body in the wedding photograph would remain for the bride as the ultimate identification with her ideal self.

My body, my responsibility

The search for an ideal body in which the individual can finally be 'herself' is attended by the risk of pitfalls and repeated failure, all of which increase the sense of guilt. The perpetual circle of self-improvement makes anxiety spiral. As Stephen Covey, the author of the leading self-help books *First Things First* and *The Seven Habits of Highly Effective People*, points out, today it is not enough to be married or employed: we must be marriageable and employable. Working on oneself (on one's body, career or identity) is the ultimate imperative for anyone who hopes not to become excluded from social networks and hopes to prosper in the job and marriage market. In the context of these new market imperatives we perceive even our own health as a marketable commodity, and this in turn has affected the way medicine is practised in the developed world. Medicine now glorifies the idea of choice and self-mastery. A doctor no longer plays the role of an authority, advising what course of action is best for the patient; now he often simply tells the patient what their options are, leaving them to make a decision and to give (or refuse) their informed consent.[13] Often this will involve a difficult and complex decision with far-reaching consequences, and without the specialist knowledge and training at a doctor's disposal the concept of informed consent may become a mockery, a way of simply avoiding responsibility and possible lawsuits if things go wrong. And do most people really want to choose what treatment they receive when they get seriously ill? While freedom of choice may seem appealing in the abstract, when things get tough, people hope that someone else – an authority, with the requisite knowledge – will choose for them. Barry Schwartz reports that, when a group of healthy people were asked whether they would want to choose between treatments if they were diagnosed with cancer, 65 per cent said yes. Among people who actually had cancer, only 12 per cent wanted to make the choice.[14]

The DIY ethic now extends to our own bodies. But the more we assume control of our bodies, the more terrifying any problem – an illness, a weakness, hospital treatment – becomes. Health problems become the individual's ultimate sin. Like the employee who is made to feel guilty for losing his job because he hasn't been able to search for a new one before the current one ends, sick people feel guilty for not preventing their illnesses. We even talk about people 'managing their stress' well! And if we can't seem to get over an illness, we feel guilty for failing in another area – self-healing.[15]

It is not surprising that the ideology of self-healing took off precisely at the moment when, in many countries, politicians began opening doors ever wider to the privatisation of public health services. Many people were becoming increasingly dissatisfied with the treatment they received in medical institutions, while at the same time it was becoming clear that in future fewer of them would be able to afford adequate and increasingly expensive private healthcare. While the ideology of self-healing promotes the view that responsibility for one's health, or even the power of effecting one's own cure, lies in one's own hands, it simultaneously fosters various new types of enterprise. Hence the plethora of New Age health gurus offering novel ways of getting in touch with one's inner healing powers.

When it comes to illness, the ideology of self-healing often leads to fantasies about what supernatural – or just nonscientific – forces are at work in the body, and what forces might be called upon to heal it. At our weakest we seek out whatever explanation and whatever help we can find. A British anthropologist who was fighting a cancer scare a couple of years ago decided to carry out a small anthropological survey in hospital by asking fellow patients how they perceived their maladies. He was very surprised by how quickly people adopt various forms of superstition when they become ill. One very educated patient, for example, believed that he could get rid of his bowel cancer if he was able to defecate; another patient tried to kill cancerous cells by drinking his own urine; and another was hoping to clear his body of his tumour by visualising that it did not exist.

People's responses towards illness have often taken various magical paths. Diseases such as the plague or even AIDS have been perceived as divine punishments, and their treatment has often included purifying rituals. In some parts of Africa, for example, it is thought that one can cure oneself of AIDS by having intercourse with a virgin.

This search for a higher power to take charge when we are at the same time insisting on our freedom to choose is not altogether surprising. When we are anxious – and choice always involves an element of anxiety (surprisingly, as later chapters will show, not about what we stand to gain by making a leap of faith, but what we stand to lose) – we often look around for someone or something to take responsibility. We may decide to consult a religious leader, a health guru or even an astrologist, in the hope of appeasing our anxiety.[16]

Recognising that the stress caused by uncertainty is a danger in itself, the Canadian Ministry of Health made several radical changes to its healthcare system. First, it decided to reorganise hospital waiting lists, after a study showed that health authorities should not leave surgical waiting lists in the hands of doctors. It turns out that doctors are likely to use the lists to their own advantage, often keeping them long in order to assure a full schedule well into the future. And a long waiting list is, after all, a sign of desirability. From the patient's perspective, though, it can induce panic. The studies showed that when patients didn't believe they would be treated in good time, with no queue-jumping, their symptoms got worse. If patients know that the system is fair, that waiting lists are managed honestly and rigorously (except in cases of absolute emergency), they are able to wait without their symptoms getting worse. And when patients are sure they will get regular check-ups, consultations before surgery and a prompt response if their condition deteriorates, the damage caused by anxiety can be kept to a minimum. In response to these findings, the Canadian government created independent local authorities to manage waiting lists and made the lists available for scrutiny on the internet. Patients' well-being improved significantly. The Canadians also realised that an efficient public health system can be a source of national pride. Finally, Canadian politicians were able to convince businesses that the public health system helped increase their profits. This was in contrast to the USA, where companies spend huge amounts of money on workers' health insurance (and where people often change jobs on the basis of the healthcare benefits on offer). In the USA, where opponents of universal healthcare continue to promote privatisation, the choices available for healthcare have already introduced a considerable level of anxiety into most people's lives.

The Big Other and choice

How is it that the simple fact of a government establishing waiting lists can reduce anxiety? And why is it that when someone appears to be in charge, or when an authority (a coach, for example) tells us what to choose, we suddenly feel more content?

The perception of what choice is varies according to the social setting. The way individuals make choices is influenced not only by what choices others are making, but also by what choice means in society at large. Lacanian psychoanalysis introduced the term the 'Big Other' to designate language, institutions and culture – everything that collectively makes up the social space in which we live. This space defines us throughout our lives, and we often create our own perception of it, picturing it as something rather coherent and full of symbols, the understanding of which we share with those who inhabit the same social milieu.

Our perception of what the Big Other is and of how it functions, however, changes over time. We complain about its inconsistencies and dream up all sorts of fantasies about what may be going wrong. When people complain that they are forced by contemporary society to choose between things they would rather someone else choose for them (such as their electricity provider), they are often confronting the anxiety either that no one seems to be in control or that all the decisions have already been made by some larger entity, such as a corporation. In other words, people are concerned about the Big Other. Lacanians believe that the Big Other does not in fact exist: the symbolic order we live in is not coherent but is notable for its gaps. It is in fact insubstantial. But Lacan's most important observation was that, although the Big Other does not exist, it nonetheless functions as though it did, since people's belief in it is essential to the way they understand their lives. In order to find at least temporary stability in terms of our identity, we create a fantasy scenario about the consistency of the social sphere we inhabit.

———

The act of choosing is traumatic precisely because there is no Big Other watching over us. Making a choice is always a leap of faith. When we try to content ourselves with self-binding mechanisms, all we are doing is 'choosing' a Big Other; we are inventing a symbolic structure that relieves us of the anxiety of choice. This is what we are doing when we put our faith in horoscopes or a charismatic politician or a god who watches over all our actions. But the very existence of the Big Other is always our 'choice', our fantasy. And by giving life to it, we choose the option of not choosing – of having our choices made for us.

People's experiences of the Big Other can take various different forms. Neurotics may have a lot of doubts, uncertainties and complaints about the Big Other, while psychotics may see it as a threat and believe that they are being harassed by voices or stalked by an invisible presence. A neurotic woman may constantly complain that no one is in charge, that the boss is a fraud, that her husband is impotent, that politicians are corrupt, that there is no authority holding society together. While the neurotic is concerned that no one is actually in charge or that the authorities are powerless, the psychotic may complain about the menacing power of authority. He may claim that his boss is following him and steals his ideas, that God is communicating with him and sending him secret messages or that politicians are plotting against him and threatening his very existence. Neurotics are bothered that the Big Other does not exist as a coherent and powerful enough whole. To solve this inconsistency, they often engage in a game of searching for a master who seems to be in charge (and thus appears as a consistent Other), while at the same time they try to undermine the master's authority. Psychotics, by contrast, do not have such concerns. They often exude certainty and have a fixed perception of what the Big Other is: a menacing gaze or a haunting voice. In thrall to such a projection, the psychotic appears to be standing outside social space with the Big Other as a material entity that exerts special power only over him.

Recently there has been a debate about how our perception of the Big Other has changed. Is this the result of a change in the mechanics of capitalism? Or is it the product of a decline in the master narratives of the last few decades, the weakening of the authority of state, church and nation? Is it because of these changes that we find it so difficult to make choices? And if our dominant ideology of choice is part of a greater change in the Big Other, how does this change affect the individual?

A decade ago the French legal theorist Pierre Legendre foresaw catastrophe: 'We do not understand that what lies at the heart of ultramodern culture is only ever law; that this quintessentially European notion entails a kind of atomic bond, whose disintegration carries alongside it the risk of collapsing the symbolic for those generations yet to come.'[17] Referring to psychoanalysis, Legendre pointed out that a subject's entry into language involves an act of separation. This separation can first be understood as a separation of the infant from their primary care-giver (usually the mother), but this separation also involves an internalisation of prohibition through speech – in other words, the cultural transmission of the law. Alongside this, every separation involves an aside (*écart*), a representation of emptiness. Because of these acts of separation, society and the subject need to find ways to deal with the category of negativity.[18]

In this context, a question emerged over whether Western culture had given up on 'introducing the subject to the institution of the limit' and had simultaneously given up on the category of negativity, at the same time as creating an ideology that puts the subject under constant pressure to enjoy – to alleviate any feeling that there might be something missing from their life.

What does it mean when we hear philosophers like Legendre saying that we live in a world without limits, or when psychoanalysts speculate that more and more people are living without internalizing social prohibitions[19] or when sociologists argue that people feel insecure and unhappy precisely because they have far too many choices in their lives? Do we really live in a limitless world? Before we attempt to answer this question, we need to explain what we mean by a limit.

One of the cornerstones of Lacanian theory is the idea that by learning to speak we undergo a process of symbolic castration, and that we are marked for ever after by a lack. The agent of castration is language itself. When we become speaking beings, something radical changes for us: 'natural' acts become much more complicated, and our existence per se appears to be devoid of some primordial *jouissance* or blissful pre-linguistic enjoyment.[20]

We suddenly need to use language in order to deal with our wants, and soon afterwards we also need to deal with desires and drives that have no primal links to biology, but which nonetheless radically affect our well-being. Language and culture, which we encounter when coming into the world, soon become not only ways of expanding our horizons but also a space of prohibition and limits to what were, at the beginning, still natural impulses. One of the prohibitions we encounter is the prohibition on close (incestuous) bonds with our primal care-giver. In a patriarchal setting this prohibition is often transmitted via the father. But the prohibition does not come about from a simple 'No!' restricting the close relationship between a mother and a child. For the prohibition to be instilled in the child, the father himself does not even need to be present, since what is crucial is the way prohibition is part of the very discourse with which a mother (or another primary care-giver) addresses the child. That is why Lacan, when referring to symbolic law, uses the term 'Name-of-the-Father'.

Although the lack that marks the individual is perceived as the loss of some essential *jouissance*, it is actually a cornerstone of subjectivity. Because the individual is marked by a lack, he or she will constantly try to recuperate the object that they perceive to embody the lost enjoyment that will make good that lack. The very fact that people are marked by a lack is thus the engine that keeps their desire alive. Thus we endlessly go on searching for the thing we hope will bring satisfaction – be it a partner, a child or a simple consumer item – and often feel dissatisfied by our choices. At the same time, however, we often feel that other people are experiencing the *jouissance* that we are searching for, which in turn provokes envy or jealousy.

When dealing with this lack, the individual encounters a further set of problems: the Big Other, itself, after all, is lacking. The social symbolic order, too, is inconsistent. Other people are also marked by lack. Thus, there is no consistent Other which will be able to appease the individual and provide an answer as to what kind of an object he or she is for this Other. And so the individual finds himself constantly interpreting, reading between the lines of what others say and guessing about the meaning of other people's gestures. The most anxiety-producing dilemma for the individual becomes how he or she appears in the desire of the Other.

These are all ordinary worries that people have in regard to the lack that marks both them and the social symbolic order. Has anything changed in today's capitalism?

In the early 1970s Lacan argued that in a developed capitalist society people think about the social world in a different way. In this 'Discourse of Capitalism' we have come to think of ourselves as masters; we believe not only that we are in charge of ourselves but also that we can somehow recover our lost *jouissance*.[21]

What is the significance of all this power? First, we appear to be no longer subject to our history or genealogy, and thus are free of all recognised markers. We think we can choose not only the objects that will bring us satisfaction but also the entire direction of our lives. In other words, we choose our particular self. Second, we behave as though, by making the right choices, we can actually come close to this forever fleeting and lost *jouissance*. The perception thus emerges that the subject is an all-powerful being who is capable of directing his or her life in the way he wishes and is capable of locating objects of desire and the *jouissance* related to them, which will bring satisfaction at last. Happiness appears to be within our group, and it is up to us to do everything possible to seize it.

Lacan wondered whether this 'Discourse of Capitalism' represents a rejection or, better, a foreclosure of castration. This foreclosure comes when society abandons all limits in order to make a push towards limitless *jouissance*. There is no longer a symbolic father to establish the rule of law. The drive for *jouissance* at all costs leads to all kinds of toxic mania and excess – alcohol, drugs, shopping, workaholism.[22] Capitalism frees the slave and makes him a consumer, but limitless consumption will end with the consumer consuming him- or herself.

This pessimistic line of thought has prompted a debate about whether capitalism actually affects the nature of subjectivity. Do people in capitalist societies experience new psychological symptoms? Has the radical change in the very nature of social prohibition and in our perception of the symbolic order contributed to an increase in levels of psychosis in developed capitalist societies?

How has the Big Other changed?

The French psychoanalyst Charles Melman sees the change in today's perception of the Big Other as related to the assumption that the world is *rationally* organised.[23] He argues that the belief in a rational world sometimes pre-empts any possibility of thinking about the Other, as well as imagining that the world is unpredictable and that there is no grand scheme that holds it together.

More than a decade ago, two other French psycho-analysts, Jacques-Alain Miller and Eric Laurent, specu-lated that there is no Big Other any more and pointed to our obsession with ethics committees as proof of this.[24] Scientific progress has raised as many questions as it has answered, and we no longer trust in any authorities to provide these answers. So we create temporary, ad hoc structures – for example, ethics committees, designed to help us deal with the inconsistency of the Big Other. These, of course, always bring their own inconsistencies.

But do we really need to be concerned about the changed structure of the social order in which we live? The French philosopher Dany-Robert Dufour feels that it is a concern and has traced the history of our percep-tion of the Big Other. Starting from Freud's supposition that each culture forms subjects who try to discern the always specific footprints leading to their origin, Dufour contends that this is 'why one paints the Other, sings it, one gives it a form, a voice, stages it, gives it represen-tations and even a super-representation, including the form of the irrepresentable'.[25] The Other supports for us what we cannot ourselves support, thus providing the ground on which we are formed. This is why our history is always the history of the Other, or rather, of images of the Other. Dufour further points out that the subject is always subject to the Other, which in the past has taken many forms of some kind of big Subject – from God or the King through to physics and 'the people'. In the course of the history of the West the distance between the individual subject and this big Subject grew smaller. Dufour identifies the moment when the individual becomes self-referential at the beginning of the Enlightenment. This was the moment when the subject stopped referring to an outside Being – God, land or blood – to confirm his existence and became in some way his or her own point of origin. With modernity, a plurality of big Subjects emerged. This is linked to the decline of the power of the Church and the vast expansion of scientific progress. Alongside this, the human subject became more and more decentred in regard to himself.

Dufour concludes that in postmodernity there is no more symbolic Big Other, that incomplete entity that constitutes an 'authority' to which the subject can address a demand, pose a question or present an objection. In such a society the market becomes the Big Other. Following Walter Benjamin's prediction that capitalism would function as a new form of religion, some today argue that the market has become God: until the recent financial crisis anyone opposed to the dogma of the free market economy was labelled a heretic.

The human subject is permanently decentred now;

the symbolic space around him is ever more anomic and diffuse. And so discussions of postmodernity have focused on the disappearance of grand narratives and reliable authorities. Individualism has reached a new stage in which the subject increasingly perceives him- or herself as a self-creator.

Problems with late capitalism

Clearly our self-perception has changed, as well as our perception of the Big Other. But can we say that the trend to promote self-creation, which I examined earlier, has contributed to a rise in psychological problems and especially to an increase in psychosis, as some psychoanalysts claim?

In Lacanian psychoanalysis psychotics are those who do not observe the same social prohibitions as most people. The so-called Name-of-the-Father, the social symbolic law, has been foreclosed and 'castration' has not been operative in the upbringing of a psychotic. Psychotics have their own view of reality; they have not, in Freud's famous formulation, agreed to give something up in order to be part of society.

French psychoanalysts today claim they are examining ever more cases of so-called 'non-triggered psychosis'. In these there is none of the delirium that normally indicates psychosis. The Polish-born psychoanalyst Helene Deutsch's idea of so-called 'as if' personalities is being revived in order to describe such cases, which are also commonly referred to as 'borderline personality disorders'. An 'as if' personality is a person who may not actually develop a full-blown psychosis of the kind suffered by Freud's patient Daniel Paul Schreber (who believed he was being turned into a woman), but they may nonetheless show signs of an underlying psychotic psychic structure. Some analysts call such cases 'ordinary psychosis' or 'white psychosis.'

What distinguishes these individuals from neurotics is that they live without doubts.

The telling case of a male patient who had a number of successful careers in his life can serve as an example. When he was young, this man befriended a lawyer in a prominent firm. He then became a successful lawyer himself. Later he met a sailor on the street and followed him into the merchant navy. He encountered a businessman and soon afterwards became one himself, with great success. Unlike Schreber, this man was not suffering a delusionary form of psychosis triggered by a particular event. Instead, his psychosis consisted in a series of successful identifications in which he not only mimicked other people but also used these powerful identifications to transform his whole life, without experiencing any apparent anxiety or doubt about these transformations. When his psychoanalyst asked the patient why, given his success, he felt it necessary to enter analysis, he replied simply, 'My wife told me to do so'. In analysis he played the role of a very dutiful patient, since once more he was trying to identify with the person closest to him.

In 1956 Lacan defined the 'as if' as a mechanism of

imaginary compensations. People with 'as if' personalities are prone to imitation. They may have problems
with their identity, such as an interweaving of identity,
or illusions of doubles. One of the features of psychotics is that they are obsessed with mimicry, shaping
themselves according to one set of ideas and then just
as quickly abandoning them, while simultaneously identifying strongly with other people. Quite often psychosis remains untriggered until the relationship with the
figure the person has a strong identification with goes
awry. For example, a young boy may not show any overt
signs of psychosis throughout his school years, since he
is strongly attached to a close friend whose behaviour
he mimics. A crisis may then occur when this other boy
moves away, for example, to college in another town. This
could provoke the end of the identification and trigger a
psychotic breakdown. Although the first boy's psychotic
structure was already in place, it was not visible until he
showed signs of delusion or disturbed behaviour as a
result of the traumatic triggering event.

Psychotic breakdown may also be provoked by a
change in the symbolic nature of a particular relationship.
In the case of one brother and sister who had a particularly
strong bond, this happened when the sister got married.
The fact that she had taken on a new symbolic role meant
that the relationship between brother and sister had
changed. This in turn precipitated a crisis for the brother,
who ended up being hospitalised after a nervous breakdown. A similar case involved a young sports star who
was in the finals of a major international competition.

Becoming a world champion would have meant a major change in her standing among the group of athletes she strongly identified with. As a winner, she would have attained a new symbolic status within the group and outside it. The girl could not cope with this prospect, and just before the tournament she withdrew, having developed serious delusions. She was hospitalised as a result.

Can we then say that the modern self is out of touch with reality, delusional in some sense? Can we argue that late capitalism is producing more psychosis? There is certainly some evidence that our self-identification is becoming more flexible. Those involved in role-playing games on the internet rarely appear as themselves, preferring in many cases to change not only their gender and sexual orientation but also their race, religion and age. There is nothing new about fantasising about being someone else, but modern trends suggest that something more profound is at stake. For instance, in the 18–25 age group in the UK, not only do more young people today report having had a sexual experience with both a person of the same sex and of the opposite sex, but they are also unwilling to classify or categorise their sexuality on the basis of sexual practice. The distinction between gay and straight appears to have little significance for these young people, when it comes to categorising themselves and others. As one commentator remarked, 'Homosexuality is over!' [26]

However, refusing to be categorised and playing with your sexual identity are not in any sense the same as Schreber's delusion that he was being turned into a woman. Schreber had no doubt about his bodily transformation. It is also not the same as the mimicry in the case of the 'successful patient' described earlier, whose transformations caused him no anxiety or uncertainty. Those of us who ceaselessly remake ourselves in the present moment have many doubts and are often overwhelmed by a fear of failure. Playing around with identifications is categorically different from the psychotic who mimics other lives, convinced that he or she inhabits someone they are not. The psychotic's certitude is replaced, in most contemporary people, with something that looks more like a neurotic celebration of the undecided.

So there is little proof that contemporary society is increasingly psychotic. Unlike psychotics, the majority of people still worry about how others see them and about how they should interact with others. Indeed, this is perhaps one reason why we have seen the increasing obsession with self-help books, which teach people that, in order to be able to have fulfilling interactions with others, they first need to learn to love themselves. However, loving ourselves is no simple matter. A search on amazon.com tells us that there are 138,987 books that will try to help you love yourself, including one called *The Learning to Love Yourself Workbook* – which shows that labour of one kind or another is as important a part of capitalism as ever.

The crucial problem may be that in a culture which so emphatically promotes self-love, loving someone else has become increasingly difficult, even if one still hopes to be loved by others.

3

LOVE CHOICES

'Hooking up' has become a common romantic ritual on US university campuses. Anxious parents can be forgiven for associating the term with 'hookers' or any of the many other subversive connotations that the phrase carries. Hooks invariably lead to crooks. A glance at the dictionary confirms that hooking onto something or someone can also suggest an unwanted attachment, enticement or deception. A hook is sometimes covered by a lure, a trick, whether it belongs to a fisherman or a sales rep. There is often a predator and a victim, a hooker and a hookee. Whether it is a footballer or a boxer, in the world of sport the recipient of a 'hook' is rarely in a happy position. Being continuously hooked, meanwhile, even if the addiction in question is healthy exercise or charity work, never comes without an undertow of enthralment, a loss of free volition. It suggests captivity and dependence. Once you are hooked, you are tossed onto the bank to die.

These readings suggest there may occasionally be something a little more ominous in 'hooking up' than is suggested by the way the term is used among today's students. For them, hooking up is never anything more than a light attachment. 'Let's hook up!' means 'see you around' or 'let's meet again at a time we choose not to specify now'. There is an expression of positive feeling towards the other person, but no commitment is made. It may be this unwillingness or inability to commit that brings the darker side of 'hooking up' into play. While 'hooking up' has an aura of casualness, it can nonetheless result in deeper entanglement. Yet the person who gets more emotionally attached than he hoped to be in the first place cannot easily admit this to himself or to his casual date. If he were to admit it, he might be perceived as someone who does not observe the 'rules' of casual encounters.

The casual encounter has taken on a primary role in American and British life. When I first visited the USA and my colleagues at the university said 'Let's have lunch', I used to take my diary out of my bag and start looking at possible dates. I quickly realised from my companions' expressions, though, that I was behaving inappropriately. It took no longer than that moment for me to grasp the correct protocol. Future eating arrangements were not really under discussion. When someone says, 'Let's have lunch', the proper response is: 'Great. Yes, let's have lunch. Call me when you're free.' 'Let's have lunch' is thus just another version of 'How are you?' The addressee is not supposed to answer with any meaningful detail but simply to respond with an optimistic 'Great' or possibly 'And how are you?' These are polite forms, designed to establish superficial boundaries. Real arrangements are reserved for the people one actually does hook up or have lunch with: those on whom one uses the formula 'Are you free for (lunch/coffee/dinner/a movie?)', specifying a particular time.

Contemporary dating rituals follow a principle of avoiding intimacy and concentrate on the mechanics of contact. 'Hooking up' serves as the supreme example. This very choice of expression reveals much about the perception of sex and love in the time of tyranny of choice. Enjoyment is no longer about searching for a spouse or a friend, coming close to the chosen object or trying to comprehend or penetrate his or her often unsettling otherness. It is about taking gratification from the process of hooking – enticing, seducing, trapping and then discarding – *unhooking* – and searching for a new object. This lack of commitment is the new vogue in relationships.

Dating as choice

The search for a mate has always followed particular social norms. A century ago, courting might have begun with a young man seeking the right to call at the home of the girl he was interested in. If and when he did call, the girl's mother or members of her family were almost always present. During the Second World War, 'calling' was replaced by 'going steady'. The constant possibility that the man would be conscripted required a ritual with a little more commitment built in, as though going steady could allay the anxiety of possible loss that war invoked. After the war large numbers of people went to college, and it was at that point that dating suddenly came to prominence as a form of courtship. The influence of parents was replaced by various types of peer pressure. New courtship rituals evolved, based on hierarchies invented by the students themselves. There was fierce competition, for example, between young men to date the women universally recognised as 'A list' and to establish themselves as alpha males by going out with them.[1] The sexual revolution in the 1960s, and the arrival of women in the workforce led to an expansion of the feminist movement and a loosening of the old rules of courtship. The idea of sexual liberation played a significant part in the changes in sexual encounters between people. When homosexuality became more socially accepted, other sexual norms became more flexible and inclusive.

'Hook-up' culture is all about choice. We have so many options in every aspect of life that the choice of emotional attachment is not only an added burden but also an impediment to the total freedom we are meant to value. Someone who gets attached too quickly has not fully profited from that freedom.

Proponents of hooking up will claim that the ritual mostly helps people to avoid getting attached too soon and that it allows people to make the best possible choice of future partner.[2] Young women especially need to protect themselves from too much investment in the encounter or too quick a commitment to the partner, they argue.[3] By keeping their options open, they will be able to focus fully on their careers and be more flexible in their future decisions. Hook-up culture is thus supposed to be about women making new rules. They are finally able to behave in the way men have behaved so often in the past. They can pick someone up randomly for a night and afterwards behave as though nothing has happened. They make no promises, and they make no demands. And since they do not want to be hurt again and again, they try not to invest too much emotion in the encounter.[4]

The paradox, though, is that in spite of this insistence on choice and control, the hook-up culture thrives on uncertainty. It may have been 'invented' to free young people from attachment, but it increases feelings of insecurity, anxiety and guilt. To appease these feelings, the ritual very often incorporates alcohol. It makes the aftermath easier. If things don't go as well as you had hoped, you can always tell your friends: 'I was drunk, I didn't know what I was doing.' Hooking up allows for anonymity, non-commitment and non-responsibility. Just as we can have many enjoyable chats with our 'friends' on the internet and have very little desire actually to meet them in person, so we can have semi-anonymous sexual encounters with people without feeling the need actually to get to know them. As one young college student put it: 'You can act as if it never happened.'[5]

Similar forms of denial exist in internet communication, where people are entirely free of restraint: they can launch vicious attacks from the safety of their bedrooms that would never be tolerated in the real world. The moment someone hits the 'send' button, an aggressive text zooms out beyond their field of vision, and thus beyond their area of responsibility. Again, he or she can behave as if the exchange never happened.

The lack of consideration – for others or for consequences – that defines hook-ups and internet encounters has a lot in common with the way we saw people dealing with financial debt earlier. Just as a person who runs up a huge credit card bill can ignore the consequences at the moment of making a purchase, so they can behave as if nothing has happened after a hook-up encounter or a bout of internet bullying.

Choice as self-protection

Since the ideology of choice has taught us that we can control our own emotions and always make rational choices, it follows that we should be able to guide our romantic relationships to produce the greatest possible happiness.[6] And yet our culture prizes the idea of romantic love precisely because it's not a rational matter. Tragic love stories are all about the suffering of two people who cannot help loving each other, who can't contain their passion. This is love beyond rational choice. It is about desires, drives and fantasies, which are all prerequisites for elevating another person into an object of supreme attraction. We fall in love with behaviours, appearances and mannerisms that appeal to something we often don't recognise in ourselves. Love has a lot to do with the unconscious choices we make that can wreak havoc with our rational intentions.

The Hollywood film *Laws of Attraction* exemplifies this conflict between rational choice and irrational attraction. It plays on the old cliché that 'people don't know what's good for them'. A high-class divorce lawyer, Audrey (played by Julianne Moore), decides to give up on romance. One day in court she notices a lawyer she finds attractive, Daniel (Pierce Brosnan), who is representing the other party in a divorce case. Audrey does everything she can to appear indifferent to his advances. Even the fact that they end up in bed together does not seem to undermine her determination to stay single. Her feelings finally change when the two are on a trip to Ireland: after a night of heavy drinking they wake up and realise that they have accidentally got married. Although it later comes to light that this marriage was a sham, the event changes something in Audrey's perspective. It is as though she is only able to recognise her attachment to Daniel after the intervention of the law – that is, after the public proclamation of marriage. Although she objects at first to finding herself in a position of non-choice, it is clear that the 'marriage' has made her happy, which is why she seems disappointed when she realises that the marriage ritual was actually a sham. When she thought that she had ended up married against her will – that is, when her choices were taken away from her – she was able to admit to her desire. In the end, she decides to marry Daniel again, this time sober and officially. But this marriage would not have been possible without the lesson that came from the withdrawal of free choice. In matters of love, the film tells us, choice may actually come only retrospectively.

When we are confused about love, we usually ask

for advice. In *Laws of Attraction* Audrey's mother offers plenty of unsolicited advice, urging her daughter to seduce Daniel. The mother belongs to the generation that embraced liberal attitudes about love and sexuality in the 1960s, while her daughter has chosen an almost celibate, career-oriented life. Rather than testing the moral boundaries of parental authority, she has installed self-prohibition to counteract her mother's permissiveness.

People have always struggled to find someone who can give good advice on love. When psychoanalysis was in its infancy, Freud was asked by a friend whether he should marry a particular woman. When it comes to the small matters in life, Freud answered, one should think long and hard, but when it comes to the big ones – whether or not to marry, whether to have children – one should just go ahead and do it. This answer sounds profoundly paradoxical, and it should be read in the context of the much more conservative society that Freud lived in. Still, the idea can be liberating if we accept that our choices in love and family are seldom rational. No matter how much we think we choose our direction, more often than not it's our unconscious desires that are in control.

Current bestselling books about love and dating suggest that we do not want to deal with unconscious desires and fantasies that pertain to love. So many of these books try to teach us about how choice should work in matters of love. Books with titles like *How to Choose and Keep Your Partner* or *Love is a Choice* give quick, rational solutions to the complicated question of seduction, and they try to show how desire can be deliberately summoned and carefully controlled. The self-help market is flooded with books about how to make someone fall in love with you, how to prevent someone from leaving you and how to manipulate someone into giving you what you want. It sometimes appears as though choice applies only to the person seeking advice, and that the goal is to take it away from the prospective partner.[7]

Choice as ideal and ideal choice

Choice in love is particularly problematic today, since we are forever chasing the ideal mate. Sometimes the search for love follows the same pattern as the search for a phone service provider: constant switching, followed by the feeling that you may have missed a better deal once you've made your choice.

This anxiety over how to make an ideal choice is present in a particular way in the former Communist countries too. Here the idea that one is supposed to be able to make choices in every area of one's life was propagated only after the introduction of capitalism. I noticed this anxiety a couple of years ago when I was invited to give a lecture in Lithuania. After some days of socialising with my hosts, I realised that they were all women. Quite a large number of well-educated, interesting women were involved with organising my visit. When I talked to these women, I was deeply impressed by how many jobs, children and intellectual pursuits they were juggling. But I was curious: where were the Lithuanian men? The women explained that men had fallen prey to the idea of choice. Their reasoning was that, when capitalism came to their country, people were bombarded with the idea of choice. Everything they wanted suddenly appeared possible. Many men thus chose more lucrative careers than academia, and quite a number of them traded in their old wives for new ones, a trend that contributed to the drastic rise in the country's divorce rate after the fall of socialism. When these women – many of whom were divorced – blamed choice for the fact that there were no men in the groups organising intellectual events, they were concluding that Lithuanians simply do not know how to make choices; in particular, they thought that Lithuanians do not know how to choose between what is valuable and what isn't. My interlocutors tried to convince me that whereas Lithuanians had only recently been introduced to the idea of choice and were dazzled by all the possibilities that were suddenly opening up, Americans had been born into a society that teaches people from an early age about the idea of choice. Of course, if one asked American women what they think about choice, they might express anxieties very similar to those of the Lithuanians.

The concept of an ideal choice is especially powerful with internet dating. Here one can see the same logic that is at work in the market-place. It's not just that people make a list of the qualities they want in a partner: they also want to cast themselves as having a particular market value. In her analysis of internet dating Eva Illouz points out that in this context the idea of the market, which has always been implicit in the dating game, has suddenly come out into the open. People want to make the best deal possible: they search for someone they imagine comes with a higher 'price tag' than themselves.[8] The internet thus in a new way instrumentalises intimate relationships by looking at them through the imagined 'value' one has in this cyberspace love market.[9]

In internet encounters a particular logic of desire is often in play. People browse for a while and see what wonderful potential partners are out there, and their standards rocket. They imagine that everyone they can see is on offer and available to them, regardless of whether or not some of them are 'out of their league'. But when the love-seeker sends out a message and gets a favourable reply, his interest plummets. At that moment self-doubt steps back in and a question presents itself: 'Why would such an attractive person be interested in me? There must be something wrong with her.' Behind this is an instinctive feeling that other people too are always in search of something better than what they currently have, and are thus endlessly trading one relationship for another.

The abundance of choice and the interchangeability that characterise internet dating reflect the dominant principles of every market in post-industrial capitalism. The ideology of efficiency, selection, rationalisation and standardisation that organises people's work lives is reflected in their highly customised dating lives. Illouz points out that the internet also introduces an interesting disparity between people's expectations and their experience: 'The Internet renders one of the essential components of socialisability far more difficult, namely our capacity to negotiate *with ourselves* the terms on which we are willing to enter into a relationship with others.'[10] When we approach dating with a wish list and then quickly assess how a potential partner matches, we are not allowing ourselves to develop a connection that might have side-stepped our rational mind.

Despite the particularly contemporary preoccupation with assessment and rational choice, internet dating actually revives a rather traditional view of love.[11] Rather than meeting spontaneously, out in the open, where we know nothing about each other, we have imposed screening mechanisms that serve the same purpose as marriage brokers and family connections in the past.[12] But meeting in reality is another matter. At that point the rational conception succumbs to unconscious fantasies and desires, and the ungraspable *jouissance* is finally at stake.[13]

Love anxiety

One of the timeless dilemmas of romantic relationships is that a person will often love in the other what the other does not actually possess – some sublime thing that the lover perceives in the beloved and out of which he creates a fantasy that keeps his love alive. But the fascination with a non-existent sublime object can quickly turn into disgust, which is why love and hate are the two sides of the same coin.[14] At the start of a relationship we may be particularly enchanted by our beloved's voice or fascinated by her quirky way of playing with her hair. When the fascination ends, we may find the voice horrible to listen to and the gestures irritating. Things that at first played a part in our feelings of love can later contribute to the collapse of the romantic bond.

The erotic deadlock in today's society arises directly from our attempts to eliminate the anxiety that love provokes and to alleviate the uncertainty that will always accompany desire. We will always wonder about exactly who we are for others and worry about what they really want. In romantic relationships these dilemmas especially trouble neurotics, who often try to find solutions to their difficulties by forming love triangles. These triangles may exist only in the mind so that, for example, an obsessive is in bed with a woman and fantasises that he is actually making love to someone else – either another woman he knows or perhaps a celebrity. In a similar situation a hysterical woman may fantasise that another woman is in bed with her man, or that she herself is in bed with Brad Pitt. If her partner is fantasising at the same time about Angelina Jolie, then there is a certain comic harmony to the situation.

An obsessive neurotic fears that by coming too close to the object of his desire he will be devoured by the object, or made to disappear. In order to protect himself, he creates all kinds of rules, prohibitions and obstacles, which become the cornerstone of his love life. For example, an Argentinian psychoanalyst once treated a man who had been sitting by the phone for a couple of nights waiting for the woman he loved to call. At that time, in Argentina, phone lines were often out of order, so the man was constantly picking up the phone to check whether it was working. So, by engaging in his obsessive ritual, the man actually prevented the woman from getting through to him.

Obsessive neurotics have various personal strategies for keeping the object of their desire at bay, in order to prevent the danger of having their carefully crafted existence disturbed. Obsessive rituals thus serve the purpose of self-protection and often result in the person enclosing himself within a solitary existence. Hysterical people, in contrast, often try to provoke the desire of admirers but then quickly appear uninterested in them. Since they are searching for the confirmation of who they are through the reactions of others, they need to keep the desire of others alive, which is why they like to appear hard to get.

In today's highly individualised society the protective mechanisms of obsessional neurosis and hysteria seem to be present to some degree in the population at large. The inability to form long-term love relationships is on the rise. In trying to establish why this is so, some psychoanalysts have asked whether changes in society have increased the incapacity to love and to open oneself up to the troubling questions posed by desire. Do we still have a space for sublime, romantic love, or have we turned into a narcissistic culture less concerned with love and desire than with finding quick, temporary sexual satisfaction? The search for the latter is more about an attempt to recover some lost *jouissance* and less about a desire to engage with another as a person, which is why the feeling of loneliness often kicks in when the encounter is over.

The French psychoanalyst Jean-Pierre Lebrun brings another element into play here by questioning whether people today have more of a problem with how to address sexual difference. He asks whether the changes in the process of socialisation have contributed to increased concern about one's sexual identity.

Every human being, when going through the process of socialisation – that is, when he is being marked by unwritten social prohibitions – takes on a sexual identity that, of course, does not necessarily correspond to his biological sex. Psychoanalysis refers to this process of socialisation by the term 'symbolic castration'. The point is not that the person becomes physically castrated but rather that, when language, cultural rituals and prohibitions 'operate' on the person, the latter becomes marked by a lack. Even the sexual identity that the person eventually takes on will not help him to deal with this lack, but will only create a whole set of new questions about his desires and drives. Lebrun asks whether current social changes have led to changes in the process of symbolic castration. In a society where authority has grown lax, there seems to be a turn towards androgyny and bisexuality. Similarly the form in which our sexuality presents itself seems to have become more narcissistic. Lebrun's pessimistic conclusion is that sexuality is becoming more and more 'a matter of competitive rivalry and consummation, it does not concern anymore a choice of a stable object. It is primarily a matter of seduction.' [15]

The hooking-up culture bears this out: we seek out someone to enchant and seduce, only to dispose of them when we find a replacement of equal or greater worth. The seducer's power comes into force at the moment when she gets a positive response. But she keeps her target at a distance: she does not want to think of the target as having his or her own desires and fantasies. When the seducer encounters such desires and fantasies, she will try to pretend that nothing has actually happened. She thus protects herself from having her own fantasies shaken up, or from being exposed as an object in the desire and fantasy of the other. Behind this attempt to appear untouched by the romantic encounter, however, is also a wish to keep the desire of her temporary partner alive. By distancing herself from him, she hopes to gain a higher value as the sublime object of desire, which can never fully be possessed.

For Jacques Lacan the appeal of Don Juan was that he could never be possessed by a woman. Women fell for him precisely because they knew that he could not be kept. Each woman could create her own fantasy about him without worrying that he might destroy the fantasy by settling down with her. A similar logic of potential availability is at work in hook-up culture. A person will not only act like she is available to numerous temporary suitors but will also make it clear that she will do her utmost not to become involved. She will seem, at least on the surface, to be in total control.

Love and prohibition

In the midst of total freedom of choice matters of love and sexuality can at first seem liberating. What could be better than the idea of total freedom from social prohibitions when it comes to sexual enjoyment? How wonderful finally to stop bothering about what parents and society at large see as right and normal! How liberating to change our sexual orientation or even the physical appearance of sexual difference!

In analysing human desires psychoanalysis has always linked desire with prohibition. When someone is suffering because they can't have what they want, the solution is not to get rid of whatever prevents them from having it, but somehow to teach the person to 'cherish' that very limit and to see that the object of desire is appealing precisely because it is unavailable.

Today very little seems to be off-limits when it comes to sexuality, aside from paedophilia, incest and rape. There is an overwhelming propulsion to enjoy. Sexual transgression is marketed as the ultimate pleasure. The idea is that if one works at improving one's sexual performance, learns new tricks and then practises them relentlessly, there are no limits to the satisfaction a person can achieve. *Cosmopolitan* encourages those who have not yet mastered the latest pleasure techniques to enrol at sex school. Yet alongside the marketing of enjoyment, the popular media also tell us about the loss of sexual excitement in many established relationships. John Gray, the author of *Men are from Mars, Women are from*

Venus, now writes about 'Why my Grandmother seems to have more sex than I do?'[16] His answer takes the form of more advice: be more relaxed, and follow this or that strategy for arousing desire. Prohibitions have always been with us, and they persist today, but their patterns have changed. If, in the past, prohibitions were transmitted through social rituals (like initiation rituals in premodern society and paternal prohibitions in traditional patriarchal societies), today the individual sets his or her own limits. She is both self-creator and self-prohibitor.

Social prohibitions will always bring with them some form of dissatisfaction. We often complain when there are barriers to our satisfaction: when we want to own a particular object we can't afford, for example, or when we are in love with someone who does not return that love. But strangely, when the obstacles to our satisfaction cease to exist and we get what we wish for, we may also have the feeling that this is not what we wanted at all and begin to search for something else. Such manifestations of dissatisfaction are an intrinsic part of how desire operates.

In a society that promotes limitless satisfaction and self-fulfilment, but which nonetheless thrives on dissatisfaction (we would not be such passionate consumers otherwise!), the sense of frustration poses new problems. For the individual, frustration is often more painful than dissatisfaction. The latter may be intertwined with desire, but frustration is linked to our problems with *jouissance* – to the very way we enjoy. Jean-Pierre Lebrun writes that 'when the will to *jouissance* dominates the social field, the brotherly solidarity of proletarians is replaced by competition and competitive rivalry. Which is where exacerbation of social hate emerges.' [17]

One aspect of contemporary racism that is rarely discussed, for example, has to do with how people object to the way others enjoy themselves. People may complain about other nations or races being too loud or having smelly food, or they may mock their presumed excessive sexual practices. Behind these complaints is the fear that others may have access to some *jouissance*, to a boundless pleasure outside their own reach. This in turn provokes a particular kind of frustration or envy. Here it is not simply that we feel dissatisfaction at the fact that others possess something that we want: we object to the very way they enjoy. This frustration over the presumed enjoyment that others experience can quickly turn into violence. It is not that we want to take from others a particular object of desire; we want to ruin their presumed enjoyment and debase them as human beings. In personal relationships our attempts to reach imaginary peaks of pleasure often end in failure. We cast the partner off in response. Frustration has kicked in, and our inability to find *jouissance* results in violence towards another. We may then try to find this lost *jouissance* with the help of addictive substances or make up for our lack by going from partner to partner.

Science as the cure for our anxieties

One way of delimiting our choices is to have recourse to the new 'science' of dating. Helen Fisher has become famous for the idea that one should study people's serotonin and dopamine levels in order to find out which character traits may go together to form a happy relationship. Her research informs the mechanisms of the dating site Chemistry.com (eHarmony.com uses something similar), which, through extensive questionnaires, attempts to assess a person's character and the underlying make-up of their brain. The reasons themselves, 'Chemistry' and 'eHarmony', let us know that the search is driven by the idea of a perfect fit.

The whole notion of the 'perfect fit', however, may well be a myth. People regularly construct fantasies around what they see in the other. Lacanian psychoanalysis calls the sublime object in the other the 'object small a'. It isn't anything that actually exists in the other or even in ourselves. It's merely a stand-in for the very lack that defines us. It is this fundamental lack in ourselves which mobilizes our desires and enjoyment. Our fantasy about what exists in the other is what makes love possible. Lacan points out that in love we give what we do not have, and we see in the other what he or she does not have. What supposedly scientific research such as Fisher's is trying to grasp is precisely the nature of this lack. But by trying to find 'certainty' in measurements of dopamine and serotonin, the research is not so much giving up on the logic of the fantasy as re-interpreting it by recasting it in today's language of science. We will always create a story around the sublime quality that we perceive in someone else, because we will never be able to grasp the nature of our attractions (or our hatreds) rationally. These new narratives, whether they rely on horoscopes or on neuro-chemical balance, are not so different in their logic: they try to give a name to whatever marks us as individuals, an element that always defies description.

Whether in rational or unconscious choice, some-thing is always lost when we choose. Those diagnosed with a fear of commitment are often just afraid of giving up an option they would have to forgo by choosing. Some of these people may have a hard time giving up a prohibited libidinal object (the mother, for example). Others may have a problem giving up the very fact that their subjectivity is always incomplete, marked by a lack. Since nothing will ever be able to fill up the lack, there is some relief in keeping all possible replacements at bay, so as to keep the search alive.

Although fear of commitment may hardly be new, of late it seems to have been elevated to the level of an ideal. Plurality of possibility increases the belief in this ideal, and partnership is pushed back further and further into the future. The result of all this choosing can well be that one ends up with nothing – as a single man or a woman. Even middle-aged people invoke a fear of commitment to explain their wandering between partners. Two suc-cessful British middle-aged stockbrokers once described to me why they were always changing their girlfriends. The first explained that he couldn't eat the same food every evening. The other man then joked that, when they bump into each other some years down the road, when both are old and lonely, they will be able to say: 'At least we always kept our options open.'

4

CHILDREN: TO HAVE OR HAVE NOT?

'Let's Make a Baby! An extraordinary and loving story of
one woman's longing to start a family', read the headline
in *The Observer* magazine. Inside was a feature about a
middle-aged woman in search of a man to impregnate
her. Jenny Withers was described as a 'happy, single and
soulful' 41-year-old woman who had never before given
any thought to pushing a pram in the supermarket, so
terrified was she of the 'mundane and domestic'. But then,
all of a sudden, she was overwhelmed by the desire for a
child. Tired of dysfunctional relationships, exhausted by
her self-centred life and apparently cured of her neuroses by years of therapy, Jenny decided to take action. She
didn't want to raise a child entirely on her own, as she
would have to if she used an anonymous sperm donor,
Jenny started searching for a man willing to give not only
his sperm but also a commitment to some ongoing role
in the life of the child. She almost convinced a homo-
sexual couple to help her, but when this couple split up,
she brought her case to a journalist from *The Observer*.

What does Jenny want? Anyone responding to her
quest is asked to send a photo, a CV and a letter explaining why he wants to be her co-parent. Jenny has criteria
of her own:

> I envisage a co-parent as being middle-class, professional,
> and with values similar to mine. Age and ethnic origin

aren't important. Physical characteristics don't matter that much, although obviously I'd prefer an attractive father for my child. In fact, the only thing that really matters are shared values. Whether he is gay, straight or in another relationship is irrelevant. I just want someone who's willing to be a father and a co-parent. I would also like him to offer some financial support.

It reads like an advertisement for a job. Although she claims to be very open as to the type of man, she clearly has some very particular ideas. Specifically, he should be a male version of herself: middle-class, attractive, with the same values. With this double, this male alter ego, she would establish a contract she rightly calls 'divorce before marriage', designed to clear away all potential areas of conflict (other children, other partners).

Jenny falls into the category of the 'new realist' moth-ers-to-be. They have seen what it's like to raise a child alone (after, for example, being impregnated by an artifi-cial donor) and decided to go another route. Jenny hopes to find someone who will help her raise the child, but she wants to be in total control with regard to the role this person will play. She will prepare for any contin-gency, and she's even thinking about hiring a therapist to help the child deal with the arrangement when the time comes. But no matter how careful her planning, she'll eventually have to accept that the other people involved (the child and the co-parent) will no doubt have expecta-tions and desires that conflict with hers.

Jenny's case is extreme. But a similar standard for rational control has for some time been part of the ideology of the American women's organisation 'Single Mothers by Choice'. The organisation brings together women who have become single parents deliberately. Their desire to have a child presumably did not involve another person. Even if they later become part of a couple, the very fact that they originally embarked on motherhood while single entitles them to membership.

But how much is reproduction a matter of rational choice, and how much does it involve unconscious mechanisms? How much can we be in charge of our desire or our partner's desire, as well as that of our parents and of society at large, when we decide whether or not to have children? And how does a society's attitude to choice affect the way people reproduce?

From rights to choices

The question of choice in reproduction has been with us for a couple of decades. An important source of choice for women in the West was the invention of the contraceptive pill, which enabled women to separate sex from reproduction and to have more control over their own bodies. But quite apart from the medical technologies available to control our reproduction, our perception of what it means to have children is heavily influenced by the particular cultural setting in which we live. When I grew up in socialist Yugoslavia, abortion was widely available and contraception was free. Growing up, I learned that the decision whether or not to have children is a personal one. But this freedom to choose was not so liberating when I faced the question myself. The time never seemed quite right to have a child. There were always other things to do first: books to write, visiting professorships to accept, apartments to buy, places to visit. I asked my doctor to tell me how much longer I could wait. I asked my friends who had children whether they ever regretted their choice. I tried to work out whether those who didn't have children were content. I was trying to make an ideal choice.

After the political situation changed, the decision whether or not to have children was presented by right-wing nationalist parties in black and white terms. Women had the right to choose between motherhood and a career, but motherhood was the right choice. In Croatia, President Franjo Tudjman even went so far as to propose that the right to abortion should be in order to enhance another right – the right of each family to have the desired number of children.

On the issue of abortion rights, Communist countries changed their views many times. Some regimes allowed abortion, realising that complications from illegal abortions were keeping women out of the workforce. Others (Ceauşescu's regime in Romania, for instance), prohibited abortion in order to increase the population.[1]

Sadly, numerous countries around the world today still deny women the right to abortion. In those countries where there has been a long history of public debate about abortion, there has been a subtle ideological battle over the difference between choice and rights. In the

USA, for example, after the 1977 Hyde Amendment took away Medicaid funding for abortions for poor women, in the public discourse on the subject the term 'the right to abortion' slowly became replaced by 'the right to choose'. Often imperceptibly, the language of consumerism started to penetrate reproductive debates, leaving political dimensions that are associated with the use of the term 'rights' more and more at the margins of public discussion.

In her analysis of abortion rights in the USA, Rickie Solinger points out that the use of the term 'choice' was laden with class content from the beginning. Middle-class women who had trouble conceiving were seen as privileged. They had many options to deal with their unfortunate situation. They could explore expensive forms of assisted reproduction, they could pay someone to bear their child, or adopt. Poor women, in contrast, lacking the financial wherewithal, did not have such options available to them. But when a poor woman did have children, this was often regarded as financially irresponsible – in other words, a bad choice. Teenage mothers and unmarried poor women were often encouraged by the medical profession to stop reproducing or give their children up for adoption. Forced sterilisation of poor women of colour and Native American woman went on in some US states even after the passing in the early 1970s of a law prohibiting this practice.[2] In public debates about reproduction rights it became clear that only women who had financial resources were accorded legitimate access to socially validated motherhood, while women who did not have those resources were deemed not to have the same maternity rights.[3] In the case of poor mothers on welfare, the choice was more complex. On the one hand their decision to conceive was portrayed as unfair to the child; on the other, it was seen as a particular economic choice that allowed the woman to receive state support. The perception was that a middle-class woman would not decide to have a child unless she could afford it, whereas a poor Black woman would get pregnant in order to qualify for welfare payments.[4]

In the context of conservative criticism of the welfare system, then, poor women were poor because they made bad choices. They also failed to embody the ideal of the legitimate consumer which had been built up in the USA from the 1960s on. Perceived as exploiters of the welfare system and thus a burden on society, they were also seen as people who did not contribute to the rapid development of consumer society. Since so many of them had neither jobs nor money, poor women were not able to consume as much as was thought desirable for the prosperity of the country.

Rights and choices evolved further in the 1970s: foetuses were granted rights, and fathers were also understood to have special rights in regard to their children. At the same time the idea of children's rights began to develop. Yet, as Solinger points out, women in the USA were only granted 'choice', which is 'rights lite'.[5]

Choice and surrogacy

Since, in the American imagination, the poor woman's choice to have a child was increasingly seen as a bad one, at various stages of the public debate on ways of limiting such choices proposals emerged for sterilisation, for long-term use of contraception and, especially, for adoption. Middle-class women, however, were perceived as being able to afford to choose not only to have their own biological child but also to adopt a child or fund a surrogate from women who were not seen as capable of making rational choices.

Take the example of the middle-class journalist Alex Kuczynski, who, because she herself was infertile, decided to hire a poor surrogate mother, Cathy, to bear her child. Alex begins the chronicle of her experience with this observation:

> As the months passed, something curious happened:
> The bigger Cathy was, the more I realized that I was
> glad – practically euphoric – I was not pregnant. I was in
> a daze of anticipation, but I was also secretly, curiously,
> perpetually relieved, unburdened from the sheer
> physicality of pregnancy. If I could have carried a child
> to term, I would have. But I carried my 10-pound dog in
> a Baby Björn-like harness on hikes, and after an hour my
> back ached. Cathy was getting bigger, and the constraints
> on her grew. I, on the other hand, was happy to exploit
> my last few months of nonmotherhood by white-water
> rafting down Level 10 rapids on the Colorado River, racing
> down a mountain at 60 miles per hour at ski-racing camp,
> drinking bourbon and going to the Superbowl.[6]

Alex further justifies her joy in out-sourcing her pregnancy by pointing out that she herself would not have been good at it, and that her body and psyche would probably have suffered too much, while Cathy was simply better-suited. Cathy even likened herself to an 'Easy-Bake oven', saying that being pregnant was no real bother for her, physically or emotionally. Cathy's decision to bear a child for another woman can be seen as an ultimate exercise of choice, the choice to commodify her own body for her own personal gain. However, she herself offered a different explanation of her act. Being pregnant for someone else let her be seen as a giver, someone capable of making another woman's dream become reality.

Cathy created a particular fantasy of what it meant to be a surrogate mother. It was not just the idea of receiving money for her work, but the perception that she was going to do a good deed for someone else. One wonders what kind of personal story was behind this fantasy. Was it something in Cathy's upbringing? How did she regard the child that she was bearing? Was it a gift that she needed to continue giving? And to whom?

The idea of the gift of a child often has a particular symbolic value for the surrogate mother. It may be enmeshed in religious and sacrificial fantasies or in the feeling that she is repaying some kind of burdensome unconscious debt to a particular person in her own past, to whom in fantasy she is offering this gift of a child. For the surrogate mother the very fact of pregnancy is itself full of possibilities. On top of seeing the process of bearing a child as a gift to another woman, she may also derive particular enjoyment from her altered body or from the status that a pregnant woman has in the family and in society, or she may even derive a painful satisfaction from her ability to go through the separation from the child when she gives him away.

As for Alex, her account of hiring a surrogate mother can be read as having a slightly exploitative tone. It depicts surrogate pregnancy as a type of labour that liberal-minded people should out-source. Just as one hires a person to do things on our behalf in other walks of life, so a busy, wealthy woman can look at surrogacy as a treat a good consumer can give herself.

How to choose oneself through choosing a child

Choice in matters of reproduction, however, does not only involve parents choosing whether or not to have a child. When they choose to do so, they also need somehow to 'choose' to become a parent. They need to identify with the role of the mother or father. Sometimes they never quite make this choice; a mother, for example, may act more like a sister to her daughter, or a father may decide that he is not willing to take on the paternal role.

The public spectacle of a tragic search for the father has become all too common. The *Maury Povich Show* on US television offers people a free DNA test whenever there is a dispute over paternity. But being recognised as a biological father and taking on the role of a father as care-giver are two very different things. Problems also arise when a woman chooses to bear a child from the sperm of a dead man: in such cases, the nature of consent from the father comes into question. In France a legal dispute emerged over the right of the child to bear the deceased father's name, when the mother used his frozen sperm to become pregnant. In Israel a court ruled that parents could use their dead son's sperm to inseminate a woman he had never met. The parents argued that such a ruling would allow the family line to continue. Although there had been no written expression of the son's desire to become a father, his family claimed that this had long been his wish. In a similar case, a US court ruled that, after a 21-year-old-man was killed in an accident, his mother had the right to keep his body preserved in such a way that doctors will be able to harvest his sperm at a later date. The mother claimed her son had told her that he wished to have three sons of his own, and that he had even chosen names for them. In order to fulfil this wish and to keep a part of her son alive, she had appealed to the court. In cases such as these, when the sperm of a dead man is used for artificial insemination, often the ideas of choice and right are reinterpreted in a new way. The woman (or the parents, in the Israeli and American cases), often cites the right to have a child from the sperm of the dead man, and the courts speculate on what this man's choice would have been if he were still alive.

In the case of children conceived from the sperm of dead men, one might also ask how they will be able to distance themselves from the dead fathers whose

memory they have been created in some measure to perpetuate. Will they see themselves as harvested people, a
kind of replica of the dead man? It may very well turn out
that some of these children will be weighed down by the
fantasies of those who brought them into existence. They
may also wonder if they were desired in their own right
and may feel angry that they had no choice.

Particular kinds of fantasies are often present in the
choice of a child's name. The French philosopher Louis
Althusser, for example, was deeply affected by the fact
that he was named after a dead man. As a young woman,
his mother had been in love with a man named Louis.
When this Louis died tragically, she married a man she
did not really love and then decided to name their son
Louis. The choice marked the young Louis for ever; he
felt like a stand-in for a dead lover. So in this case, too,
a mother who could not deal with loss tried to keep her
beloved symbolically alive by having a child who was a
surrogate for that person. The problem, however, was that
the boy who took on this symbolic role as replacement
for the old flame lost the chance to have his own identity
and to be loved by his mother, other than through a connection to her lost lover.

The struggle to make choices in matters of reproduction is an increasing dilemma today. Sometimes people
try to come to terms with these dilemmas by forming
the most elaborate of contractual arrangements. In the
USA two gay men decided to have a child by finding one
woman to donate the eggs and another to bear the child.
The couple decided that the 'genetic' mother would be

allowed to contact the child only when the child reached the age of six, while the 'birth' mother would only be able to see the child briefly after giving birth. Such a complicated arrangement tries to diffuse the problem of who is the mother, and to limit her potential claims on the child. While the couple hope to solve the problem rationally, they will never be able to control the way the child creates his or her own fantasies and dilemmas about the mother's role in his or her existence.

Psychoanalysis recognises that there are many aspects of a person's decision to have children that cannot be explained in terms of rational choice. First, the decision may be heavily influenced by one's parents. Behind a woman's or a man's desire to have a child may very well be the desires of his or her mother or father: a son might thus present his child as some kind of a gift to his mother. A daughter might diminish the parenting role of her partner (the biological father) by placing the grandfather in the role of the most powerful paternal authority. A woman might insist on having a child because she wants proof of what she means to her partner. She might say: 'If you love me, you will have a child with me.' She is not expressing her desire for a child, but rather questioning her partner's desire for her. A man whose partner demands a child might very well find his love for her diminished after the child is born. He may have idealised his partner before and felt he loved her deeply but, when she became a mother, found that his unconscious desires towards his own mother came to the surface. His own mother is, of course, off-limits as a love object, and when his partner becomes a mother she takes the role of that prohibited incestuous object. Freud pointed out that some men solve this dilemma by splitting the object of their love into a virginal, idealised woman (who is off-limits) and a whore (a woman whom the man debases, but whom he can also sexually enjoy).

Many cases of women searching for a sperm donor illustrate the desire for an idealised person who will for ever be inaccessible. *The New York Times* reported that women who search for sperm donors nowadays first request all kinds of information about the donor (his academic results, his smile, his physical build). Occasionally these women fall in love with their idealised donor, and the fact that he is inaccessible only strengthens their feelings. However rational a woman's choice of a particular donor may seem, this choice always touches intricate levels of desire. She may also pick a donor who resembles her father or her lost lover, or a donor who will offer no competition for the child's love. She may pick one because he will somehow be for ever hers: since he is out of reach, the fantasy she has about him will never be shattered by reality.[7] There is no way of knowing, however, how the child will respond to the diverse forms of desire his mother felt on bringing him or her into existence.

From desire to demand

A recent case of octuplets being born in the USA sparked new debates about choice and demand in reproduction.

The very fact that mother of the octuplets, Nadya Suleman, was a single mother who already had six children, all conceived through in vitro fertilization (IVF), raised the question of whether there should be a limit to how many children one can conceive through assisted reproduction, and especially how many fertilised eggs can be implanted simultaneously. At the time of her last IVF treatment Suleman was implanted with six of the fertilised eggs left over from her previous treatment. (Two of these eggs later divided – hence the eight children.) Suleman answered by saying: 'Those are my children, and that's what was available and I used them. So, I took a risk. It's a gamble. It always is.'

All she ever wanted, Suleman said, was to have a big family. She was an only child who felt little connection to her parents, and as an adult she wanted to repair this damage by becoming a devoted, loving mother. Her mother, Angela, pointed out that Nadya turned her boyfriend into a sperm donor for all fourteen children, but refused to marry him: 'He was in love with her and wanted to marry her', Angela said. 'But Nadya wanted to have children on her own.' It is important to point out that Nadya Suleman is a religious woman, which is why all of the octuplets were given Biblical names. When asked whether she ever thought about the fact that she doesn't have the resources to provide for such a large family, she said: 'I just kept thinking God will provide.'

Suleman's case raised a variety of questions about the limits of choice in reproduction. How should the medical profession impose limits, if at all, on a patient's demand for IVF, particularly in cases when the patient already has so many children or is in some way incapable of providing for them? Should there be a limit to the number of fertilised eggs one can have implanted at one time? (Since implanting many fertilised eggs carries a strong risk for mother and children alike, surely doctors should be obliged to warn of the potential risks.) Should the sperm donor (the biological father) have the right to impose a limit on how many times his sperm can be used in the process of insemination? And should there be a limit on how many children he can father, or with how many women?

If we examine these questions through the lens of psychoanalytic theory, the question is whether we are dealing with some underlying psychotic structure. When someone has this insatiable desire for more children, what do the children symbolise for them? In Suleman's case people were troubled to see that she regarded these fertilised eggs as extensions of herself, elements that were not to be wasted, and that she never questioned how her donor might feel about this. Nor did she consider how her children might respond to her choice to have so many. A number of commentators pointed out that Suleman's face looks strikingly similar to Angelina Jolie's and that she may have undergone plastic surgery in order to achieve that resemblance. Since Jolie's family is also expanding rapidly, the identification suggested a deeper identification.

Psychoanalysts have observed another significant shift among the desires of middle-aged women to conceive. A working woman may be anxious about her career prospects; a married woman may worry about how having a child will affect her marriage; a single woman may wonder how she will cope with a child on her own. Such anxieties may send women to psycho-analysis to help them decide whether they really wish to have a child at all. There the patient may have to face the issue of how she was desired by her own parents. And sometimes she will find that she was not desired at all and was in some way, directly or indirectly, rejected. The prospective mother will obviously hope to avoid making the same mistake.

But a peculiar shift from desire to demand has taken place. Instead of wondering whether they are ready and able, patients now declare a demand for a child. A woman might say: 'I want to have a child. It is my right to have one, but my husband is preventing me.' Sometimes she may see a doctor as obstructing her right.

The ideology of choice has guided this turn from desire to demand. This raises the question of what effect this will have on future children. It is one thing to approach the question of how we were desired by our parents, but quite another to accept how they 'demanded' us. The woman who 'demands' to have a child may very well believe that the child will make her in some way complete. She may have difficulty separating herself from the infant, which in turn could prove suffocating for the child.

In cases when a child is conceived with the aid of a donor, the mother will also need to explain her choice to the child and create a narrative of why she decided to reproduce in a particular way. The child may very well then pose a number of questions related to the father. The mother will need to endure these questions and offer solace by stressing the very fact that the child was strongly desired and that, while the biological father is not present, the child is loved by a number of other people. In a television interview Nadya Suleman admitted that her older children ask about their father every day. Her answer to these questions is to say that she will reveal the identity of the donor when the children reach eighteen. But when that time comes, they will then be confronted by the 'choice' of whether or not to try to track down their father. Burdening one's children with such a possibility may provide the mother with an easy way out of a difficult dialogue. The father/donor, however, does not seem to have any choice in regard to how his life has turned out after he donated his sperm to a friend.

Troubled decisions

Many women who struggle with a conflict of desire in deciding whether or not to have children often confront, consciously or unconsciously, the question of how they themselves came into this world. Some women point out that they have pondered the nature of their own mothers' desire and that their decision to have (or not to have) children has been influenced by how they have interpreted their own mother's desire to have them.

In her interviews with women who had trouble deciding whether to have children, the American psychotherapist Phyllis Ziman Tobin found that a number of
them traced their uncertainty back to their own mothers'
ambivalence. This was especially the case with women
whose mothers were dealing with the conflicting cultural stereotypes of the 1960s and 1970s. Although a large
number of American women were entering the workforce at that time, the notion of the housewife remained
the ideal. Many women pointed out that they were afraid
of change, and of the loss of control change brings. They
were worried about the change to their bodies and to
their lifestyle; they were anxious about being responsible for a baby. Some wondered what the term 'mother'
actually meant: how is a mother supposed to behave, feel
and look? 'I don't want to look dumpy like my mother',
was a common refrain. The idea of what a mother looks
like meant something very different for these women
who had trouble deciding whether or not to have children. One patient, Jean, said both her mother and grandmother were depressed after childbirth. She was worried
about continuing that cycle. This was compounded by
the fact that her mother had told Jean that she had sacrificed herself for her children by staying home, and that
she was happier when she went back to work as a teacher.
Another patient, Diana, could not deal with the risk of
being left all alone with her baby, as her mother had been
with her. The fear of loneliness was coupled with the
fear that her marriage would collapse if she had a child.
Reflecting on these worries, Diana realised she did not

want to repeat her mother's story of frightening away her husband and then ending up miserable and divorced. For her the decision whether or not to have a child was closely bound up with her sense of what she represented for her own mother. But when Diana's husband was diagnosed with cancer, she finally decided to have a child. The issue of loss had emerged in a new way: if the fear of loss at first prevented her from having a child, later this same fear prompted her to become pregnant.

When a woman finally decides to have a child but is then unable to conceive, she suffers another trauma. She loses the feeling that everything is possible. In today's ideology, which promotes the notion of 'having it all', that loss leads directly to a feeling of powerlessness.

Choice in reproduction is a powerful tool. Although the choices we make about having children are often entirely unconscious, we cannot give up on the power that comes from knowing we have choices. Even when women find that they are unable biologically to have a child, they can still sometimes comfort themselves by thinking that this is their own choice. It is not uncommon for an infertile couple to continue using birth control even after they have learned that they cannot conceive. It is a sign that they still consider reproduction to be a matter of choice.

On every side of the question of whether or not to have children, people confront loss. They confront the fear of losing their autonomy, overloading a relationship, losing control, losing their figure or their own inner child. On the other side, the decision not to have a child brings the loss of an imagined future, of a yearned-for bond with another, an idea of continuing the family line or a gift to their parents or partner. It can even bring the loss of a narcissistic image – the image of their own younger self in the face of their daughter or son.

5

FORCED CHOICE

In considering who and how to marry, what to do and
where to work, where and how to live, alternatives abound:
in each case we face the very different worlds that each
decision will open up. The most painful dilemma, though,
comes when more is at stake than just the immediate
outcome for the decision-maker. Major life choices not
only create alternative futures; they also reinterpret our
past. Mihnea Moldoveanu and Nitin Nohria, professors of
business administration who specialise in human motiva-
tion, write that 'our anxiety about deciding does not stem
from a secret wish to hold time still, and thereby become
timeless and immortal, but from the unfulfilled wish to
harmonize what is with what could have been'.[1] Then, of
course, there are the choices which at the time seem incon-
sequential, but which in retrospect prove to have changed
everything. For today's choice-enabled person, it is not
only the multiplicity of possibilities that brings anxiety, but
the fear of loss. In taking a risk we tend to give more weight
to what we may lose more than what we stand to gain.[2]

Robert Frost's poem 'The Road Not Taken' epitomises
this problem of choosing, so when M. Scott Peck took
a line from it as the title of his popular self-help book
The Road Less Traveled, he was drawing on the resonance
of the twentieth century's most famous and ambiguous
meditation on choice.

Two roads diverged in a wood, and I –
I took the one less travelled by,
And that has made all the difference.

Deciding on 'the road less travelled' sounds like a brave idea – it epitomises the ideology of risk-taking, of standing alone and heading down the solitary path. Yet the road not taken will continue to haunt us. To resist the nagging doubt, we spin out a story, a narrative, to support the choice we made, recalling portents and distinguishing features of the options we had. But in fact, as with Frost's two similar tracks in the wood, we may have seen no difference at the time.

The choice that presents itself to an existential being in the twenty-first century is a choice between two very similar-looking paths. The fact that a choice of such apparent slightness can have vast repercussions is what makes us anxious. Everything depends on a seemingly chance turn, even though we may subsequently tell the story of bold choices made in situations where foresight, in truth, was impossible. Through a compensatory, selective act of memory we generate the idea of a 'road less travelled'. It lends an element of heroism and forbearance to a course of action that may have been taken casually at the time. And it lends glamour to the path not taken. We can ease our unhappiness with what is and what was by summoning thoughts of what might have been. A source of real despair lies in the thought that there might have been nothing for us but boredom and discontent, no matter which road we took. This is a thought, incidentally, that comes closer to the Calvinistic sense of doom that haunted Robert Frost.

Impossible choice

If Frost's poem is about a curiosity concerning what might have been if another choice had been made, together with a tinge of regret over the loss of this possibility, today, at the start of the twenty-first century, people often deal with the impossibility of making any choice at all. When there are so many options to choose from, when choice becomes so overbearing, and when the responsibility for making the wrong choice appears so anxiety-provoking, foundering in indecisiveness seems to offer protection from the possible regret and disappointment that choice might provoke. Unlike Frost's man in the woods, today's individual is facing not simply two roads to choose from, but a crossroads where many roads meet. When there are so many possible directions to take, and when it is so important to take the right one, the individual can endlessly procrastinate, seek more and more information about the various options and, in order to preclude the possibility of failure, never make up his mind at all.

Faced with an overwhelming array of possibilities, people find thousands of ways to avoid making choices. In a book provocatively titled *Should You Leave?* the American psychiatrist Peter D. Kramer shows how people deal with choices related to their love lives.[3] Anyone who has ever been in a long-term relationship has at one time or another dealt with Kramer's question. Some brush it off immediately, some ponder it for years. The key variable is just how loud and pressing the question becomes. But many of us simply deny that the question arises. Someone can persuade herself, for example, that staying in a relationship is the only option consistent with her identity, or she can justify staying by using the opposite rationale – that even if she leaves nothing will actually change. In both cases she convinces herself that there actually is no choice. We can also deny the fact that our actions often have irreversible effects. So she might leave but then think that she can undo what she's done by going back. This too is a denial of choice, assuming that, although we took one road, we can still go back to the other. The love story we abandon will continue, as it were, even in our absence, and so we can refuse to deal with loss after we have decided to leave. We can preserve the illusion that some change is just around the corner. 'I can leave tomorrow', 'I am free to do things differently.' We may never actually leave, but entertaining the possibility that we might do so allows us a fantasy of radical change without ever compelling us to choose, and to accept the loss. We thus do everything to postpone choice or make it impossible.

In his analysis of the master–slave dialectic Hegel points out that a master risks his life in exchange for public recognition. The slave forgoes recognition in exchange for certainty about the future. A person who avoids choice acts more like a slave – clinging to certainty even at the price of being trapped in misery. Anxiety over

the unknown can be harder to bear than the contingencies of the known.

Choice can be impossible, however, not only in situations that involve a step into the unknown, but also in cases
where the idea of choice seems simply inconceivable. One
of the most excruciating examples of impossible choice
appears in William Styron's novel *Sophie's Choice*. At the
centre of the story is Sophie's terrible memory of the time
she spent in a concentration camp, when a Nazi doctor
forced her to choose which of her two children should live
and which should be sent to the gas chamber. The doctor
tells her that if she fails to choose, both children will die.
She keeps her son and sacrifices her daughter. She never
recovers. For a while she finds some slight comfort in the
belief that her son may have been saved, but ultimately she
learns that he too has died in the camp. In her discussion
with the doctor, Sophie hopes that she might gain some
advantage by pointing out that she is a Polish Catholic
and not a Jew. The doctor answers: 'You're a Polack, not
a Yid. That gives you a privilege – a choice.'[4] The religious
devotion Sophie hopes will save her becomes an excuse
for this particular form of moral torture. She remembers
rumours that this doctor is himself supposed to be a religious man and that as a young man he wanted to enter
the ministry. His mercenary father had forced him into
medicine. Having himself been pushed into a situation of
non-choice, the doctor may later have found particular
enjoyment in offering impossible choices to people like
Sophie. The narrator, Stingo, explains the doctor's behaviour another way:

He had suffered boredom and anxiety, and even
revulsion, but no sense of sin from the bestial crimes
he had been party to, nor had he felt that in sending
thousands of the wretched innocent to oblivion he had
transgressed against divine law. All had been unutterable
monotony. All of his depravity had been enacted in a
vacuum of sinless and businesslike godlessness, while his
soul thirsted for beatitude. Was it not supremely simple,
then, to restore his belief in God, and at the same time
to affirm his human capacity for evil, by committing
the most intolerable sin that he was able to conceive?
Goodness could come later. But first a great sin. One
whose glory lay in its subtle magnanimity – a choice.[5]

For the doctor, forcing Sophie to make the impossible choice is a way of making God operative again, to
commit a sin so provocative that God will have to inter-
vene.[6] In a sense the doctor has found a way to invite the
Big Other – the coherent order of things – back into his
life, and assign to it the kind of meaning we all miss when
confronted with difficult choices.

Psychoanalysis and choice

The ultimate dilemma of choice lies with the fact that
every human life is, in the most fundamental way,
optional. Albert Camus put it this way: 'Shall I kill
myself or have a cup of coffee?' Beyond all the little
decisions that decide what kind of life we will live lies
the question of whether to continue living at all. With
every choice we make, we pass over the option of not

making any choice at all, or of destroying our capacity to choose altogether. But if we continue living, our suffering also becomes a choice we have made. Psychoanalysis here has a radical take on the individual's responsibility for this choice, which is far removed from the idea of rational choice.

An important moment in the history of psychoanalysis came when Freud started using the term *Neurosenwahl* – the choice of neurosis. Freud came to the idea of the 'choice of neurosis' through a self-critique of his early work. At first he thought that the decision as to which neuroses people develop depends on sexual events in early childhood; later, however, he decided that neuroses are far more dependent on the nature of the repression and defences in the ego. 'It is not a question of what sexual experiences a particular individual had had in his childhood, but rather of his reaction to these experiences – whether he reacted to them through "repression" or not.'[7] Reaction is thus a form of choice, and the individual is responsible for his or her neurosis.[8] The individual is not simply a product of outside forces (society and parents, for example) but also an 'author' – a maker of his own responses to these forces. But these responses are not his rational choice; rather, they are 'choices' made at the level of the unconscious.

Jacques Lacan also perceived the formation of subjectivity (which he refers to using the term 'subjectivisation') as being linked to choice. However, choice here is not conceived as a kind of self-making: it is not rationally deciding who one is, or, making a work of art of oneself. Subjectivisation for Lacan is about the process of how the Big Other – the symbolic structure (for example, language, culture and institutions) into which the subject is born – marks the subject in a particular way. It is not simply that the subject has to go through a process of socialisation through which he will inadvertently become a social being. Becoming a subject also involves a particular moment of choice, which is not a rational choice but rather something that Lacan refers to as 'forced choice'.

Lacan explains the logic of 'forced choice' with an anecdote about three condemned prisoners. The prison warden informs the prisoners that they can escape the death sentence if they solve a particular puzzle: each of them has either a black or white disc stuck on his back. Altogether there are three white and two black discs. From these the warden has chosen three – one disc for each prisoner. While each prisoner cannot see the colour of his own disc, he can see those the two others are wearing. Each prisoner has to try to work out the colour of his own disc without talking to the others. The first to do so successfully will be set free. Now, if one prisoner has a white disc while the other two wear black, the one with the white disc has an easy task, since he will immediately see the two black discs and thus quickly conclude that he has the white one. In this case, his eyesight will be enough to win the game. Things become more complicated if one prisoner has a black disc and the other two white. The prisoner who sees one black and one white disc will reason: 'If I have a black disc, the prisoner with the white disc would have seen two black discs and thus be able to leave the room; since this has not happened, I must have a white disc.' A still more complicated detour in thought is needed if all three prisoners have white discs. Here all of them reason in the following way: 'I see two white discs. If I have a black disc, the other two prisoners must guess whether they are black or white, as would be the case if we had two white discs and one black between us. Since neither of the two others has made a move, I must be white myself and thus better stand up and leave.' In this case the prisoners' choice relies on hesitation on the part of the others. Each of the prisoners hesitates, but only by seeing hesitation also on the part of other prisoners is he able to make a gesture and stand up.

We can read this puzzle as an explanation of how the subject 'chooses' him- or herself. Everyone always feels radically uncertain about who he or she is. And taking on a certain symbolic identity (that is, making the proclamation 'This is me!') involves a detour through the Big Other. First, there is the language in which the subject is placed and in which, with the help of appropriate signifiers, the subject will take on his or her symbolic identity. Second, there is the subject pondering over desire of the Other – both the Big Other, the larger social space in which the subject lives, and other more intimate human beings. The subject is forever guessing what kind of an object he or she is in the eyes of society as such (the Big Other) and in the eyes of other people. It is through observing others and speculating about what they see in us that we try to learn who we are for them and for ourselves. And it is through trying to obtain social recognition that we hope to ascertain how the Big Other sees us. In regard to both questions – what we mean for other people and what place we have in society at large – we are constantly left without a proper answer. Others cannot really tell us what we represent for them, since they are often not rationally aware of the desires and fantasies that they form around us, and in society at large there is no authority per se that would grant us a fixed identity or that would respond to our quest for recognition. Thus we are forever left to form our own interpretations, to read between the lines and try to guess what others really say about us, what we mean to them. We also try to ascertain what kind of position we have in society at large, and when we award ourselves medals or seek social status, we hope that the Big Other will recognise our importance, although here again we will be left to interpret for ourselves what the Big Other is and what it values.

However, it is not just that we are constantly thrown into making our own choices in regard to what others are saying. The very fact that we ourselves start to speak and become members of society involves a particular choice. In order to speak, Lacan argues, we need to go through the process of alienation and loss. Lacan explains this with a diagram showing the intersection of two circles (the field of the subject and the field of the Big Other). On the side of the subject we have Being, and on the side of the Big Other we have Meaning – language, institutions, culture and everything else that defines the world a person is born into. In the overlap between the subject and the Big Other is a place of non-meaning. The subject, however, has no option but to commit to this vacant intermediate zone. There will be no meaning clear to him, none that he can make by himself. He will always guess about meaning in regard to what his culture makes of it. Lacan points out:

> The veil of alienation is defined by a choice whose properties depend on this, that there is, in the joining, one element that, whatever the choice operating may be, has as its consequence neither one, nor the other. The choice, then, is a matter of knowing whether one wishes to preserve one of the parts, the other disappearing in any case.[9]

Lacan illustrates this choice with the dilemma when robbers demand 'Your money or your life?' If one chooses money, one loses both, since one will be killed, but if one gives money, one also loses: one will have life deprived of money.

In regard to defining who the subject is for him or herself Lacan stresses the 'future anterior' in contrast to the 'past tense'. In other words, 'I will be what I am now through my choice' rather than 'I am what I already was'. Like Freud, Lacan concedes that we are all determined by our past. But we always have a choice as to how we react to that past, even though this 'choice' is perceived as a forced choice which is linked to the subject's defences. The choice is deeply traumatic in that it entails a loss and opens a void. The advent of the symbolic presented by the forced choice brings forth something that did not 'exist' before, but which is nonetheless anterior to it, a past that has never been present.[10] Through the act of forced choice we are deprived of something we never had but still managed to lose.

The most important point about all these cases of so-called 'forced choice' is that we are not dealing simply with the absence of choice. The choice is offered and denied in the same gesture. However, the very fact that we can make the gesture of choosing, although the choice itself is a forced one, accounts for the fact that the subject is not determined by external or internal forces. This in turn accounts for the fact that subjectivity always involves a certain freedom, even if this freedom is only the freedom to form one's own defences. When Freud, for example, looked at the case of Dora, the young woman suffering from hysteria who in her analysis complained about complicated family relationships, her own traumatic seduction by a family friend and other forms of personal suffering, he avoided drawing the conclusion that there was a logic of cause and effect at work in this situation. The complicated social and sexual relationships in Dora's cultural milieu were not the direct cause of her suffering. Her hysterical symptoms were her own response to the situation and to her own unconscious desires, which she could not rationally interpret. Although she appeared to be a victim entangled in other people's emotional games, she actually had her own desires invested in these games. Her symptoms were the result of these desires becoming articulated in a rather painful way; however, these symptoms were precisely the points where we can recognise these moments of subjectivisation, since these are always of the subject's own making.

In a different context forced choice emerges in the domain of politics. The army of the former Yugoslavia had a ritual for conscripts beginning their military service, a ceremony in which the young soldiers took an oath and signed a statement saying that they freely chose to become members of the Yugoslav army. Occasionally a young soldier would take this choice seriously and refuse to sign the oath. Such acts of disobedience were severely punished, and the conscript would usually be put in jail. He would be released only when he 'freely' signed the oath. Something similar happened in Baghdad, when an Iraqi man was released by the American military after spending more than two years in detention facilities, having never been charged with a crime. When he was finally released, the military asked him to fill out a form asking how he had been treated during his detention. He was asked to put a tick next to the sentence that best described his treatment. The first said that he had not suffered any abuse during detention, and the second sentence said that he had. He filled out the form in front of three American guards carrying the same electric stun devices that were often used to punish prisoners. Even the translator told the man to tick the first sentence. When the man inquired what would happen if he ticked the second one, the translator raised his hands to say he didn't know. It is not hard to imagine that if the man had ticked the second sentence, he would never have been released from prison.

In cases where someone is offered a choice and at the same time deprived of it, they are of course not given a choice at all. But forced choice still holds value as an important part of the social bond. The very fact that we have cases of forced choice suggests that society understands that everyone is capable of freedom. Society cannot simply reject this freedom. Even the most severe forms of totalitarian regime often resorted to acts of forced choice, showing that coercion can frequently be based on a fantasy of the individual's free submission to the regime's orders.

These political and everyday examples of forced choice are nonetheless different from the psychoanalytic idea that the individual has a forced choice to establish his or her defences (or neurosis). In the political examples there is a choice of action (to join the army or go to prison, to tick the 'no torture' box on the form or die, to follow the code required by an 'act of politeness' or to fail to be polite). But there is, crucially, no choice of defence in these examples. The prisoner or the conscript can save his skin but not his truth. But the Lacanian subject in the process of socialisation faces a more severe dilemma. If the subject does not make the forced choice to form individual defences, she can fall into psychosis. Yet even psychosis is a matter of choice, although again a forced one. Even in falling into psychosis, Lacan argues, the individual is responsible; a psychotic structure is not simply imposed on her but is, rather, her own formation, albeit not a conscious one.

Death and the lack of choice

If forms of suffering (our neuroses, for example) are in psychoanalysis perceived as being a matter of forced choice, what about the end of suffering – death? Our anxiety about the idea of death is often linked to two contradicting causes: first, the fact that we have no choice in regard to it, since everyone must die; and second, the fact that we do have the power to end our life by our own will. In order to appease this anxiety, religions often offer ideas about a possible continuation of spiritual existence after the body passes away. Today, however, we try to keep anxiety over death in check by inventing ever new ways to postpone death or to perceive it as something that one can control – through euthanasia, for example.

The way in which post-industrial societies deal with death again offers a version of the ideology of choice. If in the past we were powerless before what Baudelaire called the figure of Time, the sole predator who never risks anything and never operates at a loss, these days there is considerable pressure on the individual to make this figure wait. Ageing, dying and defining our place in the succession of generations have become more difficult as our freedom of choice expands.[11] Our choices seem to be timeless, as though there were no progression towards inevitable decay and death, as though life was just a matter of circling round a single spot and not a progression towards the inescapable end. The ideology of late capitalism promotes the eternal present and thus cannot easily deal with ageing and dying. The Western media present ageing as unacceptable and offer it up as a matter of choice: it's up to every one of us to do something against it, to work on concealing the signs of age and to find a way of postponing or even preventing death. This has led to our obsession with showing how death and dying actually look. Popular culture, with its endless tally of shot and murdered and dissected bodies, and high culture are both at play in this morbid terrain. Celebrities nowadays look the same throughout their lives. Their faces appear frozen in time, often at the price of an uncanny effect of a living death.

The traumatic issues that a society faces are often reflected in a revealing way in the art practices that gain importance and public recognition at a particular time. And contemporary art has for some time been obsessed with death and dying. Today, however, art often engages with mortality in a way that encapsulates society's attempts to postpone it at all cost. Alternatively, it transforms death into just another artistic creation.

The American artist Stephen Shanabrook, for example, constantly returns to the subjects of death, medicine and chocolate. He became well known for making pralines by moulding chocolate from the wounds of dead bodies that he found in Russian and American morgues. I asked Shanabrook how this combination of chocolates and dead bodies came about, and he answered with a theory about his childhood. His father was a doctor, and as a young boy Shanabrook was fascinated by surgery and the idea of his father performing autopsies. At the same time, he was obsessed with the smell of chocolate from a chocolate factory that he passed every day on his way to school. As a teenager, he started working in the factory so that he could breathe more of the smell. In explaining his art work, Shanabrook points out that chocolate melts at a temperature very close to the normal temperature of the human body. By moulding chocolates from the wounds of corpses, Shanabrook tries to deal with the horror of the wounds. The more people observe the pralines, it seems, the more inclined they are to forget the origin of their shapes and to enjoy the seductive chocolate smell. When parts of a dead body become moulded into chocolate pralines, one gets the uncanny feeling that the artist himself must have been deeply touched by death and the process of dying in his life and that with his art work he is both provoking and denying the horror associated with death.

Psychoanalysis understands such creative circulation around a particular issue as a form of sublimation. Instead of making a 'choice' of a symptom through which a person would articulate his suffering, the person engages in a professional pursuit or, in other words, sublimates his drives. This sublimation results in the production of a work of art that others can admire. This process becomes more difficult to understand, however, when there is no product to be shown other than one's own body. Here body artists are especially intriguing. When the French artist Orlan constantly changes her face with the help of plastic surgery and decides, first, to look like Mona Lisa and, later, to have horns implanted into her forehead, she seems to take seriously the ideological call to make a work of art out of her own body. At the same time, in her own way she is also sublimating her unconscious drives, which is why her constant body alteration is a particular kind of forced choice. It looks as though she has no choice but to engage in this alteration even though, of course, she has not been forced into it.

An artist who constantly changes their body and treats it as an art object is pushing the idea of choice to its furthest limits. They are, however, in their own way also reflecting on the idea of denial, which, as previous chapters pointed out, is linked to the promotion of choice in our society.

This denial can be seen at work in body art, where the body appears as an immortal machine endlessly capable of transformation. It is present also in art that deals with accidents and catastrophes. The Mexican photographer Enrique Metinides has become a well-known practitioner of so-called 'catastrophe arts', which show dying itself as an artistic practice in order to annihilate the traumatic elements of death. Metinides's rise to fame almost resembles today's reality TV shows, in which ordinary people become famous merely for being at the right place at the right time. For forty years he has been compulsively collecting images of disasters – car accidents, train crashes, suicides or fires. Like Stephen Shanabrook, Metinides could not let go of his chosen theme. And here, too, a particular childhood event seems to hold the germ of his obsession. When Metinides was twelve years old, his father bought him his first camera, and Metinides began recording the car accidents that happened at the crossroads near his father's shop. He was soon on the staff of a major newspaper, their youngest photographer, charged with recording human suffering. This practice continued throughout Metinides's life, although he eventually stopped using a camera and decided to record disasters on video, installing seven TV screens in his apartment to aid him in his work. Metinides's entire life has thus been about recording and cataloguing accidents and suicides. Through his photographs Metinides tries to transform the uncontrollable – disasters and accidents – into something that can be controlled and ordered by being catalogued. In his organizing zeal Metinides has even gone so far as to create special codes for emergency crews to identify the kinds of injury they will encounter at the scene. He also collects toy versions of various rescue vehicles, from ambulances to fire engines and police cars.

Metinides seems to have a problem with death – one that psychoanalysts often observe in obsessive neurotics. Obsessives want to be in control of every aspect of their life and especially to control death. In an interview, Metinides once said that his biggest two fears were of being buried alive and of having an autopsy.[12] His photographs often either entirely focus on the eyes of the observer and in a way neglect the accident itself or try to capture the open eyes of the dead person, so that they appear not to be dead. In a strange way, corpses in Metinides's work look as though they are still alive. He presents death as something different from what it is, in order to overcome his own horror of dying.

While art may try to deal with death's traumatic character by repeatedly showing us how it looks, in life we often try to forget this. Psychoanalysts grappling with the issue of forgetfulness have realised that it has a soothing effect. Even in clinical cases of dementia in old age, we can see that there are benefits in forgetting. Forgetfulness is related not only to events from the past but also to capability to think ahead. Dementia in old age thus helps the sufferer to forget the future and so annihilates the anxiety related to his own mortality.

For obsessives, it is precisely the issue of mortality that is unforgettable. Jacques Lacan has characterised an obsessive as someone who constantly asks: 'Am I dead or alive?' Since the obsessive is horrified not only by his own desire but especially by the desire of the Other, he first tries to get rid of this desiring Other. He can then take the place of that Other and seize the control that the other had possessed. In other words, in order to prevent anything unexpected, the obsessive becomes an Other himself. He hopes that with the death of the desiring Other, he will finally be free to live. However, by continuously imposing new rules and prohibitions on himself, he instead becomes like one of the living dead, a robot-like creature, drained of desire.

Is our society, with its insistence on choice and the seeming control that goes with it, in some way privileging an obsessive attitude to life? Rather than declaring that psychosis is on the rise, it seems wiser to conclude that the insistence on choice in every area of our life has given rise to an obsessive need for control and predictability, as well as a paralysing fear of death and annihilation. By constantly following advice about how to shape our bodies, how to curb our desires, the direction in which to steer our lives and especially how to prevent our deaths, we certainly don't gain more certainty or more control. Rather, the ideology of choice is 'choosing' the obsessive personality for us, selecting the form of neurosis that will contribute most to capitalism in its current form.

The paradox is that the obsessive attitudes promoted by the ideology of late capitalism actually leave very little room for choice. The highly controlled individual who is constantly on guard, who dreads disorder and who is petrified by the thought of dying derives very little enjoyment from playing out the supposedly limitless possibilities of choice. He is in the grip of an anxiety about failing to be the ideal 'chooser'. So he invents ever new ways of restricting choice.

CONCLUSION

SHAME AND THE LACK OF SOCIAL CHANGE

In Slovenia capitalism has transformed funeral rituals. In the past, bereaved family members would usually visit a state-run funeral parlour, where they would select one of several basic funeral services and choose from a couple of different coffins or, in the case of cremation, urns for the ashes. Today the ritual is more like a shopping experience and an occasion for shame or embarrassment. When the bereaved visit a funeral home, they are asked to decide about all sorts of details as to how the service will proceed. Most of these decisions relate to objects that will either never be visible or which will be immediately destroyed. If, for example, the deceased is to be cremated, the family must decide how elaborate and expensive the coffin will be. Then they need to decide how much to spend on the urn in which the ashes will be kept. This urn will later be buried. And in addition to deciding just how extravagant the urn should be, they have to choose between flower arrangements, musicians for the service and even the size of the announcement to be placed in the newspaper.

Why does this provoke shame? When making choices in front of a salesperson in the funeral showroom, the bereaved are exposed to two kinds of gaze: that of the person selling the services and the gaze of a non-substantial other, who appears as an abstract agency looking down from above. Here is that Big Other again, whom we have already met. Embarrassment and shame are often tied to our sense of identity. Someone may feel embarrassed about being poor, about being an 'unmanly' man or an 'unwomanly' woman, or about being a member of a particular nation. One might feel embarrassed about failing to abide by a set of implicit or explicit rules, or about failing, for example, to abide by the principles laid down by one's Big Other. A soldier may feel ashamed for not acting bravely in combat, a father may feel ashamed for not meeting his own ideal of what a paternal figure should be, or a judge for not acting authoritatively. The awkwardness one experiences when arranging a funeral ritual triggers similar feelings of failure, of not acting properly. No matter what you do when presented with the choices in the funeral salon, you fail. If one refuses to buy the extravagant urn, one may need to deal with feeling mean in front of the salesperson, but if one chooses the most expensive option, one may feel one is showing off and that such extravagance is unreasonable. Failure is inevitable. In such situations we often feel self-reproach. There are, however, a variety of ways we may combat this feeling. 'The affect of self-reproach', Freud wrote,

> may be transformed by various psychical processes into other affects, which then enter consciousness more clearly than the affect itself: for instance, into anxiety (fear of the consequences of the action to which the self-reproach applies), hypochondria (fear of its bodily effects), delusions of persecutions (fear of its social effects), shame (fear of other people knowing about it), and so on.[1]

When we are ashamed, what is it that we are afraid other people will see? It is not simply that we feel like a failure, since at a rational level we usually know we have done nothing wrong. Shame is a reminder that, by definition, we can never completely fulfill our expectations of ourselves. What we don't want others to see is that we are in essence always frauds. We may temporarily take on some symbolic role and bask in the fantasy of its permanence, but sooner or later we will be exposed, and our identity, marked by an essential lack, will be shown up as a sham.

The iconography of people feeling ashamed of something often shows them with their hangdog expressions, their eyes averted. On the one hand, they are avoiding the gaze emanating from others, but they are also trying not to look *at* the others. In many cultures one looks down when approaching a figure of authority. What is it we don't want that authority to see? We are not supposed to see others in their nakedness. We show someone respect by averting our gaze so as not to see through their façade to the lack that lies beneath. In *The Wizard of Oz*, Dorothy does exactly that when she at last confronts the Wizard.

Shame is connected to our inconsistency, to the inconstancy of the authorities in our lives and to the inconstancy of the Other. When I feel ashamed, I am not only trying to avoid the disapproving gaze of the Other, in front of whom I feel humiliated. By averting my own gaze, I am also trying not to see the fact that the Other is itself also inconstant, or rather that the Other, in the final analysis, does not exist. As Joan Copjec points out:

Shame is awakened not when one looks at oneself, or those whom one cherishes, through another's eyes, but when one suddenly perceives a lack in the Other. At this moment the subject no longer experiences herself as a fulfilment of the Other's desire, as the centre of the world, which now shifts away from her slightly, causing a distance to open within the subject herself. This distance is not that 'superegoic' one which produces a feeling of guilt and burdens one with an uncancelable debt to the Other, but is, on the contrary, that which wipes out the debt. In shame, unlike guilt, one experiences one's visibility, but there is no external Other who sees, since shame is proof that the Other does not exist.[2]

When societies impose rituals that shame their citizens, they are desperately working to sustain the fiction of a constant and consistent Other. But they are only revealing their own inconsistency. This is particularly apparent in some countries' judicial processes. In China, when a criminal is to be executed, his family is asked to pay for the bullet. The demand relies in part on the family's shame. Paying for the bullet is a form of repayment of a debt to society. But it can also be read as a sign that the judicial system alone cannot act with complete authority; it needs the family's 'help' in meting out punishment. The British government has commissioned research on how best to involve communities in the fight against crime and raise public confidence in the criminal justice system. The proposal written by Louise Casey, the former head of Tony Blair's Respect Task Force, suggests that offenders sentenced to community punishment be put to work wearing bibs that clearly identify them as criminals.[3] The public is meant to feel satisfaction in seeing criminals being punished in a socially useful way, rather than biding their time in a prison. But the bibs don't just make criminals visible to the public; they also divert the public's gaze from itself – from its own failure to deter crime.

When we feel ashamed of the choices we have made, we avert our gaze from society at large and focus on ourselves. We lower our eyes in front of social injustice and feel ashamed for not making the right choices. Rather than seeing cracks in the social order, we see cracks in ourselves and see the limits of our enjoyment and fulfilment as our own great failure. This is particularly hard for the poor, whose lives are so far from fulfilment and happiness, and who must bear the blame as individuals for their failure to measure up. In times of reality television, adventure parks and endless new forms of entertainment, being poor can be misunderstood from outside as an optional condition, a game that you can join in and opt out of at will. Just before the start of the current economic crisis one British newspaper ran a story by a journalist who had lived for two weeks as a homeless person. The journalist who embarked on this assignment wanted to know if it was possible to survive in London without money or credit cards. The story used lurid pictures of the reporter rummaging about in dustbins, sleeping in a squat, washing in a public lavatory, and crashing gallery openings and parties in search of free food. Another British journalist who finally landed a job as a newspaper columnist wrote in one of her first columns:

> I cried over a pork chop on Friday … For the past year
> I've eaten only Ryvita, value bread, value no-fruit jam
> and dried pasta … But being broke was also a blessing. In
> hindsight, my friends may travel the world searching for
> adversity and enlightenment, but I have survived being
> broke in London. Try that, I write back smugly when they
> email from India. I now ignore use-by dates, appreciate
> second-class stamps, and even use non-branded
> toothpaste.

The idea that this journalist puts forward is that enduring poverty gives one a strength unknown to those who haven't experienced it. The poor can conquer embarrassments that others dread – having their debit card declined, for example, and having to whittle the size of the bill down until payment is accepted.

On an internet site dealing with finance Donna Freeman proudly explained her decision to live on $12,000 a year. 'I've made my choices,' she said,

> And they include no more husband, a college education
> and huge changes in the way I spend money … I'm poor
> by choice, because I needed to change my life. I *chose* to
> leave my marriage, and I *chose* to become a student. I can
> live this way because I know it won't be forever. I'll have
> my degree in two more years, and I'll go back to work.[4]

So choice can be a powerful motivator when a person decides to take another path. But conservatives have long used the argument that poverty is a choice, in order to perpetuate class divisions. From the beginning capital-ist ideology relied on the idea that everyone can have prosperity and that those who remain poor just haven't worked hard enough. In the USA, Barbara Ehrenreich, author of *Nickel and Dimed*, and other authors who decided to live as poor workers for a couple of months have shown that workfare cannot simply replace welfare and that, no matter how some poor people try to take control of their lives, they cannot escape poverty by sheer will-power.

Before the impact of the current economic crisis began to be felt, the idea of consumption was so dominant that even spending less (and possibly working less) became a work task. At the beginning of 2007 a Californian couple decided to go a whole year without spending anything. They recorded their experience in a blog.[5] Simultaneously, in other parts of the USA other small groups of people got together and resolved to reduce their consumption, using the internet to declare that they would not buy any new products other than food, toiletries and basic essentials for a year. Some groups decided that they were allowed only to buy second-hand goods, and to repair old objects or rent them. A number of American writers also explored the issue of downsizing their lives. Judith Levine, for example, published *Not Buying It: My Year without Shopping*.[6] But with the beginning of the economic crisis, when people suddenly started losing their jobs and homes, these adventures into poverty by middle-class writers started to look like a cynical take on economic hardship.

The emergence of the movement for simplifying one's life in fact bought into the ideology of choice in a specific way, all the while deceiving itself and others with a moralising rhetoric. For the movement actually accepted the premises of a highly individualised society. The ideology that teaches us that everything is in our hands and that we are free to make what we want out of our lives merely repeats this mantra in the language of life-simplification. The trend to simplify one's life is in that sense a reaction to overwhelming consumer choice replicating itself in another form of consumer choice. Since a huge part of the world's population is offered very few choices and has to endure terrible poverty every day, the Western movement to simplify one's life (along with other attempts to glorify poverty) seems a rather hypo-critical way for essentially well-off people to address class divisions obliquely. Within this movement, too, the idea of rational choice dominated the dialogue. In her article 'Living "Poor" and Loving It' Donna Freedman points out, somewhat narrow-mindedly, that the most impor-tant money-management tool is one's brain.[7]

As I have argued, choice actually has little to do with one's rationality. The way someone deals with choices often reflects their deeper psychological make-up. A hysterical woman is likely to be chronically disappointed with the results of her choices. When she makes a pur-chase, she immediately realises, 'This is not it!', that she is not satisfied. She then goes off to shop for another object, rather than assessing the real cause of her discon-tent. A male obsessive, in contrast, might avoid making a choice in the first place and procrastinate instead. Making a choice would require him to act on his desire.

A psychotic might be even more paralysed, since for him it may appear that he has no freedom at all and that someone else has already chosen for him, which is why he feels oppressed and controlled.

The choices we make are often irrational. When we buy an expensive car, it may very well be in order to arouse envy, and not because we have rationally concluded that we need this particular model. Arousing envy is very much part of today's marketing. A new trend introduces humiliation into the mix. In Japan a number of stores became fashionable by limiting people's choices. One such stylish store, on the outskirts of Tokyo, has entirely random opening hours. Shoppers arrive, form long queues at the doors; and, when the shop finally opens, often find that the sales assistant will arbitrarily refuse to sell them the item they want. Shoppers are not offended. They are fascinated and flock to the stores in great numbers.

It is often hard to choose what you want to eat in a Chinese restaurant simply because there are so many options. This kind of variety has come to seem like pandering to the least discerning customer. This, at least, is the thinking behind the practice in many high-end restaurants of choosing the diners' meals for them. At Nobu customers pay huge sums for the chef to choose whatever he wants to serve that evening. Gordon Ramsay in London offers his customers the chance to eat a meal in the restaurant's kitchen. Of course, they have no choice as to what they get. In London there used to be a restaurant that did not have prices on its menu, and customers were asked to decide by themselves how much they wanted to pay for the meal. Not surprisingly, the majority paid more than was expected.

While some may try to teach people to limit their choices, my claim is that people already form their own self-binding mechanisms, although these are not developed consciously: they are not 'rational' strategies. People limit their choices by themselves, or they act as though someone else had imposed limits for them. A professor once decided before an exam to give students the chance to set the question they wanted to answer. The students did not find it liberating in the slightest. When the exam came, they were deeply shocked to be asked the very question they had set beforehand, and behaved as though they had been asked something very obscure and completely unpredictable. One student even complained that the question did not relate closely enough to the material they had been covering in the course. So although a person makes his or her own choice, he or she can easily act as though the choice has been imposed by someone else.

Desires always involve certain prohibitions. We are quick to invent new obstacles when the old ones cease to exist. The owner of the Conran shop in London knows this very well: 'People do not know what they want,' he has said, 'until you give it to them.' After September 11, when there was quite a tourist boom in Slovenia (since people perceived it as a safe place to visit), the Slovenian tourist board decided to use prohibition to increase desire. In their advertising they used the strapline 'Don't go to Slovenia!' The desire for limits can also be seen in little children. If there are too many possibilities to choose from, they get agitated and plead for guidance from their parents. Even if they end up choosing exactly the opposite of what their parents suggest, they find solace in not having to deal with limitless choice.

The very fact that we so often search for advice in our choices suggests how crucial it is that the individual find a safety net in a community – whether a virtual one or a real one. Making choices has become a very lonely act. In the past we could rely on families or other groups. Now we are on our own. Yet people find ever new ways to search for advice. I have noticed in the USA how many women in communal changing areas in the department stores ask fellow shoppers for advice as to whether to buy a particular piece of clothing. The answer of anonymous women is often very honest, much more so than that of a relative or friend. Someone we know may try too hard not to cause hurt or may respond with jealousy, or indeed simple boredom, but an anonymous adviser may be flattered to be asked and is perhaps more honest because there is no deeper emotional attachment at stake.

The New York Times reported that some Americans who had run up huge credit card bills began keeping personal blogs in which they could candidly describe what they were going through.[8] One woman would not admit to her partner or to her friends that she was in debt but, after expressing her anxiety on her blog, gradually found the strength to cut her spending and reduce her bills. The blog gave her a sense of accountability; when she is shopping, she may have it in mind that she will have to confess her purchases on the blog. In her mind the anonymous readers become guilt-inducing authorities, monitors. The nameless readers of a web page are woven into her superego, reinforcing it, and through this psychological detour into cyberspace the woman becomes far more capable of taking action than she would be by confiding in the people close to her, who fail to exert the same pressure. The fact that she felt such action was necessary in the first place illustrates the weakness of her real – that is, her non-electronic – community. It also shows how, when such communities lose their power both to support and to guide, choices are harder to make, and even why an individual in distress may find great solace (as well as pain) in compulsive shopping in the first place.

But no matter how traumatic choice is, it is an essential human capacity. The fact that a person is able to make choices opens up the possibility of change. The problem today is that we see all choice as entirely rational, and so our ideas about it tend to fall in line with economic theory and consumerism. We allow ourselves to be governed by those theories. In reality, we need a much broader psychological understanding of choice. The fact that psychoanalysis sees people as responsible for their symptoms does not mean that each of us has rationally chosen our suffering. However, it does mean that the person is a subject – someone who always creates an individual symptom (or neurosis). Change is possible, and we have the capacity to overcome individual suffering as well as to create it.

Today's capitalist society, with its insistence on the idea of choice, masks class difference as well as racial and sexual inequality. In 1987 Margaret Thatcher famously declared that, 'there is no such thing as society. There are individual men and women, and there are families.' This view has subsequently permeated every level of contemporary society. The feeling of shame for being poor and of guilt for not getting further up the ladder of economic success has replaced the fight against social injustice. And the anxiety about not being good enough has pacified people, leading them not only to work longer hours but often to work just as hard at their appearance. Choice can open up the possibility of change at the level of society, but only when it is no longer perceived as solely an individual prerogative. The success of the ideology of choice in today's society has been in blinding people to the fact that their actual choices are becoming severely limited by the social divisions in society and that issues such as the organisation of labour, health and safety, and the environment appear more and more beyond their choice. At the level of society we are therefore losing the possibility of choice in terms of change in power relations as we know them. Not surprisingly, the ideology of choice goes hand and hand with the New Age ideology that promotes living in the moment and accepting things as they are.

It is possible, however, for the struggle against the ideology of choice as the ultimate panacea for all troubles actually to use the idea of choice in a way that subverts the dominant ideology. This happened in London when groups of young people decided to fight against the free newspapers that are often pushed into people's hands when they get on the buses or tube. These newspapers are full of sensational exposés and stories about celebrities' tastes and exploits. Using the slogan 'Choose what you read', a group of opponents of these free newspapers started offering people second-hand books instead. They hoped this gesture would prevent the particular mental pollution that the free papers engender.

When any idea is glorified in a particular society at a particular time, it is necessary to be cautious about it. In Communism this happened with workers' rights and ideals of a classless society. In late capitalism this is true in relation to the idea of choice. When people were fighting against Communist ideals, the Party apparatchiks criticised them with arguments that power was already in the hands of the people and there was therefore no need to battle against the regime. Capitalism interprets choice through a similar ideological operation. Choice about the organisation of society is offered and denied at the same time. Liberal democratic capitalism glorifies the idea of choice, but with the proviso that what is on offer is primarily a consumerist model of choosing. The choice of a new form of social organisation, of different ways in which society might develop in the future and especially the possibility of rejecting capitalist society as we know it all appear not to be available choices.

As this book has argued, choice is no simple matter and often enough not a rational one. Just as choice enters our individual lives when we least expect it – which doesn't mean that it wasn't a choice motivated by unconscious desires and drives – so too at the level of society choice often occurs at unpredictable moments. When the Polish journalist Ryszard Kapuściński, in his book *Shah of Shahs* describes the Iranian revolution in 1979, he postulates as the turning-point the moment when the police were trying to stop a man on the street and he ignored them. Demonstrations followed, eventually bringing down the regime. The change was a matter of choice, but it was also unpredictable and uncontrollable. While our ideology teaches us that rational choice will help us maintain control, make life predictable and annihilate risk, the reality is that choice takes away precisely our ability to predict the future. It opens the door to regret over what might have been and opens the window of hope for what is to come.

John Lennon famously sang that 'life is what happens to you/While you're busy making other plans'. This also goes for choice: thinking about choices and making them seem to be two different matters. But we can choose whether to accept or decline the tyranny of choice – and we can begin by understanding what is really on offer.

NOTES

Introduction

1. Jennifer Niesslein, *Practically Perfect in Every Way* (Putnam Adult, New York, 2007).
2. http://women.timesonline.co.uk/tol/life_and_style/women/the_way_we_live/article2467750.ece.
3. *Financial Times* (29 and 30 November 2008).
4. *The New York Times* (28 November 2008).
5. See Renata Salecl, *On Anxiety* (Routledge, London 2004).
6. Richard Sennett, *The Fall of Public Man* (Faber and Faber, London, 1986), pp. 337–8.

Chapter 1: Why choice makes us anxious

1. Italo Calvino, *Mr Palomar* (Vintage Books, New York, 1994), p. 72.
2. See, in particular, Greg Easterbrook, *The Progress Paradox: How Life Gets Better While People Feel Worse* (Random House, New York, 2004).
3. Will Ferguson, *Happiness*™ (Harper Perennial, New York, 2003).
4. William Perkins, a seventeenth-century Cambridge theologian, developed a self-help type of thinking in his work *A Treatise of the Vocation, or, Callings of Men, with the sorts and kindness of them, and the right use thereof* (1603). Other works from the same era on the same theme include Abraham Jackson, *The Pious Prentice*, and Immanuel

Bourne, *The Godly Mans Guide*. For the analysis of these works, see Louis B. Wright, *Middle-Class Culture in Elizabethan England* (University of North Carolina, Chapel Hill, NC, 1935).

5. Ralph Waldo Emerson, 'Wealth', in *The Conduct of Life* (Houghton, Mifflin & Co., Boston, MA, 1904).

6. Written and directed by Leslie Shearing (2003).

7. Micki McGee, *Self-Help, Inc.: Makeover Culture in American Life* (Oxford University Press, Oxford, 2005), p. 11.

8. Shakti Gawain, *Living in the Light: A Guide to Personal and Planetary Transformation* (New World Library, New York, 1998), p. 145.

9. See McGee, *Self-Help Inc.*

10. Even in the family one is supposed to negotiate and schedule meeting times. An ideal parent is perceived as a family coach who is able to encourage others, support them in positive thinking and equip them with tools that help them focus on their goals.

11. *The New York Times* reported on the rise of spiritual coaching for women, where busy women can find guidance about their diet, emotions and relationships, as well as healing techniques for cancer, depression, addiction and other illnesses associated with their stressful lives. See Alen Salkin, 'Seeing Yourself in Their Life', *The New York Times*, (18 September 2009); http://www.nytimes.com/2009/09/20/fashion/20Guru.html?hpw.

12. http://fengshui.happyhomezone.com/fengshui/.

13. http:// fengshui-rockies.com. How does one get success in life? The advice given is as follows: 'The first thing that you need to do is get yourself a good compass and determine what is in the southeastern corner of your home. The southeastern sector of your home governs both your cash flow as well as your faith in the idea that you will always be able to create money. According to the classic

and traditional rules of Feng Shui (the ancient art of object placement to increase good energy in your life) the items that you place in this part of your home should be things that align with the energies of personal abundance.'

14. Barry Schwartz, *The Paradox of Choice: Why More is Less* (Harper Perennial, New York, 2005). Another book recently published on choice is Edward C. Rosenthal, *The Era of Choice: The Ability to Choose and Its Transformation of Contemporary Life* (MIT Press, Cambridge, MA, 2005). This book focuses more on the political and economic dimension of choice. My stress is on the individual's struggle with choice in their private life.

Chapter 2: Choosing through others' eyes

1. Darian Leader, *Why Do Women Write More Letters Than They Post?* (Faber and Faber, London, 1997).
2. The show was presented on MTV.
3. The show was available on iEnhance.com.
4. In the USA parents' obsession with early engagement of their children is often referred to as 'Tiger Woods syndrome'. Pushy parents who hope that with early training they will be able to make their child into a future sports star not only impose harsh training schedules on their kids but also often engage in aggression towards each other when their children do less well than expected in competitions. See http://www.msnbc.msn.com/id/4556244.
5. Bill Pennington, 'Expectations Lose to Reality of Sports Scholarships', *The New York Times* (10 March 2008).
6. http://www.drjimtaylor.com/blog/2008/08/the-dark-side-of-youth-sports-superstardom/
7. Jake Halpern, *Fame Junkies: The Hidden Truths behind*

America's Favorite Addiction (Houghton Mifflin, New York, 2007).

8. Ibid., p. 98.

9. Ibid., p. 99.

10. Ibid., p. 152.

11. Robert Phaller (ed.), *Interpassivität*, Studien über delegiertes Genießen (Springer, New York and Vienna, 2000).

12. See Pat Wingert and Sarah Elkins, 'The Incredible Shrinking Bride: How the Pressure to Look Perfect on the Big Day is Leading Some Women to Extremes', *Newsweek* (26 February 2008).

13. The idea behind informed consent is that the person wants to make rational decisions in regard to his or her health. Many studies, however, show that denial is often a very powerful tool in a patient's recovery. Israeli cardiologists, for example, have analysed the difference in survival rates of heart attack patients in terms of whether the patients were prone to deny their condition or were highly aware of it. The latter group lived a life full of precautions in regard to their condition after their attack, while those prone to denial often lived their life as though nothing had happened. Surprisingly, people who were less concerned with their health after the heart attack lived longer than those people who were forever monitoring their condition. For an analysis of informed consent see Atul Gawande, *Complications: A Surgeon's Notes on an Imperfect Science* (Profile Books, London, 2003).

14. See Schwartz, *The Paradox of Choice: Why More is Less* (Harper Perennial, New York, 2005).

15. In the history of cancer there has been a change from group concerns for healing cancer to individual ones. In the 1970s, for example, after the USA was able to land a man on the moon, a special optimism emerged in society with regard to scientific advancement and the prospect of a cure for cancer

in particular. The so-called war against cancer was begun by Richard Nixon. The idea behind this 'war' was that very soon science would be able to offer a cure for cancer. If at that time concern for uprooting cancer was related to a state initiative, later, with the emergence of heightened individualism and the lack of success in the war against it, the illness became much more an individual matter. With the power of the idea of self-healing, the individual became wholly responsible for preventing cancer and even for overcoming it once it has been diagnosed. See the book by Siddhartha Mukherjee, *The Emperor of All Maladies: A Biography of Cancer* (Scribner, New York, 2010).

16. Medicine sometimes recognises people's need to finds comfort in religion and spirituality when dealing with illnesses. In some Californian hospitals, where they treat many members of South-East Asian communities, they have now allowed visits by shamans who perform particular healing ceremonies. Doctors who supported this practice pointed out that belief affects people's ability to recover from illness in a variety of ways. Belief in the power of a shaman can for some people have the same effect as belief in the power of a drug has for others. Over half of those who respond to anti-depressants, for example, do so because of the placebo effect. See Patricia Leigh Brown, 'A Doctor for Disease, a Shaman for the Soul', *The New York Times* (20 September 2009); http://www.nytimes.com/2009/09/20/us/20shaman.html?pagewanted=print.

17. Pierre Legendre, 'The Other Dimension of Law', *Cardozo Law Review*, vol. 16, no. 3–4 (1995), p. 943.

18. Ibid., p. 950.

19. See, particularly, Charles Melman, *L'homme sans gravité: jouir à tout prix* (Gallimard, 2002) Paris, and Jean-Pierre Lebrun, *Un monde sans limite: essai pour une clinique psychanalytique du social* (Erès, Paris, 2001).

20. The English translation of the word *jouissance* is 'enjoyment'. However, this word loses the original French meaning of the term, which designates not just pleasure but also pleasure in displeasure – that is, in a certain pain that is not necessarily enjoyable to the person but which the person nonetheless cannot give up. Because of this complex meaning, the word *jouissance* is often left in French in English texts that refer to Lacanian psychoanalysis.

21. Jacques Lacan developed this theory in his lecture at the University in Milan on 12 May 1972. The original text is unpublished.

22. One type of critique of late capitalism points out that the consumer is just a semblance of an agent, following only a semblance of freedom. In reality, he or she is under the pressure of demand. This demand comes not from the Master Signifier, but from the place of *jouissance* – the 'object small a'.

23. Melman, *L'homme sans gravité: jouir à tout prix*.

24. Jacques-Alain Miller and Eric Laurent, 'The Other Who Does Not Exist and His Ethical Committees', *Almanac of Psychoanalysis*, 1 (1998), pp. 15–35.

25. Dany-Robert Dufour, *The Art of Shrinking Heads* (Polity Press, Cambridge, 2007), p. 44.

26. I am indebted to Henrietta Moore for this assessment of UK culture.

Chapter 3: Love choices

1. See Kathleen A. Bogle, *Hooking Up: Sex, Dating, and Relationships on Campus* (New York University Press, New York, 2008).

2. Ibid., p. 184.

3. Laura Sessions Stepp, *Unhooked: How Young Women*

Pursue Sex, Delay Love and Lose at Both (Riverhead Books, New York, 2007). Since relationships are messy, time-consuming and often full of disappointment, many young women decide to engage in commitment-free 'hooking up'. But, as Stepp shows, the emotional price that women pay for this is often very high since, in contrast to the purported deal of 'non-attachment', they often still become deeply involved in the relationships they enter.

4. The idea that women need to behave like men in terms of emotional attachment, and that they need to be able to separate love and sex, was already promoted in the advice books for women that emerged in the 1980s and after. With the emergence of new unisex emotional codes there is a noticeable coldness of tone in the texts about emotion written by women as advice to other women. In these texts emotional ties are viewed increasingly through the lens of business priorities. Emotions appear as matters of investment and as something that one needs to be in control of. For the analysis of this shift, see Arlie Russell Hochschild, *The Commercialization of Intimate Life: Notes from Home and Work* (University of California Press, Berkeley, CA, 2003).

5. Bogle, *Hooking Up*, p. 169.

6. An important part of some people's erotic lives is, of course, taken up with paid encounters with prostitutes. In her study of sex workers in post-industrial capitalism Elizabeth Bernstein points out that a significant shift has taken place in today's society with the emergence of the 'girlfriend experience' (GFE) type of sexual trade. In contrast to the quick sexual encounters with traditional prostitutes, GFE encounters involve extended foreplay, lots of talking and a desire on the part of the client to bring sexual pleasure to the prostitute. 'For these men, what is (at least ideally) being purchased is a sexual connection

that is promised on bounded authenticity.' Elizabeth Bern-stein: *Temporarily Yours: Intimacy, Authenticity, and the Commerce of Sex* (University of Chicago Press, Chicago, 2007), p. 127. Arlie Russell Hochschild presents the oppo-site example of a paid relationship where a wealthy man advertises for an attractive woman who for a substantial fee will perform the duties of a hostess, travel companion and occasional masseuse, but not at all as a sexual partner. Hochschild points out that today we experience a particu-lar kind of out-sourcing of emotions: 'A half century ago, we might have imagined a wealthy man buying a fancy home, car, and pleasant vacation for himself and his family. Now, we are asked to imagine the man buying the pleasant family, or at least the services associated with the fantasy of a family-life experience'. See Arlie Russell Hochschild, *The Commercialization of Intimate Life*, p. 31. Both the example of GFE and the advertisement for a companion who does not offer sex involve a particular kind of fantasy on the side of the paying male. If the man who purchases GFE creates a fantasy of the enjoying other (the prostitute), the man who is purchasing a non-sexual companion creates the fantasy of a perfect harmonious relationship that will not be muddled up with emotions (neither his nor the woman's). Both men in a similar way create an individual fantasy of the perfect partner whom one keeps at a dis-tance with the help of money. It is precisely because these women are paid and asked to perform a very particular role that the man can keep himself safe from the compli-cations that an encounter with the other often involves. For these men it is enough that in their fantasy they create their own idea of how desire of the other should appear. By doing so, they try to protect themselves from the often surprising and uncomfortable actual encounter with the desiring other.

7. Together with this ideology goes the idea that love today is supposed to have its basis in self-love.

8. Eva Illouz, *Cold Intimacies: The Making of Emotional Capitalism* (Polity Press, Cambridge, 2007), p. 88.

9. Although dating sites look like vast shopping centres, where a person can endlessly choose between possible mating candidates, people are always finding ever new ways of limiting their possibility of choice. On some Indian dating sites people are looking at all the possible class, caste and other requirements in order to limit their choice. In this case people – often parents of potential partners – are relying on old ideals when searching for a particular trait among the people on offer.

10. Illouz, *Cold Intimacies*, p. 98.

11. There has been a change in the way we assess other people in times of increase of communication. Arlie Hochschild, for example, speaks about new types of human emotional labour that we can observe in contemporary society. This change in emotional labour is related to the fact that 'a good part of modern life involves exchange between total strangers, who, in the absence of countermeasures and in the pursuit of short-term self-interests, might act much of the time out of suspicion and anger rather than trust and good will.' See Arlie Russell Hochschild, *The Managed Heart: Commercialization of Human Feeling* (University of California Press, Berkeley, CA, 2003).

12. Nowadays there are also new forms of brokers who provide temporary partners for a variety of occasions where one needs to appear in public with a partner, a friend or even a best man. A Japanese agency started providing people with such temporary partners and found an ever-increasing demand. On top of women renting men who would show up at public events and pretend to be their partners, the agency also had requests to rent men who would flirt

with a woman while on a date with her husband in order to make him jealous and prevent him from straying. See Justin McCurry, 'Lonely Japanese Find Solace in "Rent a Friend" Agency', *The Guardian* (20 September 2009). http://www.guardian.co.uk/world/2009/sep/20/japan-relatives-professional-stand-ins.

13. Some time ago in Japan technology was introduced to help single people. They could record their interests on a special device and when they met another single person with the same device who had similar interests, the device would make a sound. The idea behind this invention was that people want to meet others with similar interests. In reality, however, it is not rationally expressed interests that hold people together.

14. See Renata Salecl, *(Per)versions of Love and Hate* (Verso, London, 1998).

15. Ibid., p. 251.

16. This theme was discussed on John Gray's website. See http://www.marsvenus.com.

17. Lebrun, *Un monde sans limite*, p. 250.

Chapter 4: Children: to have or have not?

1. There is more on this in Renata Salecl, *The Spoils of Freedom: Psychoanalysis and Feminism after the Fall of Socialism*, (Routledge, London, 1994).

2. Rickie Solinger, *Pregnancy and Power: A Short History of Reproductive Politics in America* (New York University Press, New York, 2005), p. 198.

3. Rickie Solinger, *Beggars and Choosers: How the Politics of Choice Shapes Adoption, Abortion, and Welfare in the United States* (Hill and Wang, New York, 2001).

4. For a detailed analysis of race and abortion in the USA, see

Loretta J. Ross, 'African-American Women and Abortion', in Rickie Solinger, *Abortion Wars: A Half Century of Struggle, 1950–2000* (University of California Press, Berkeley, CA, 1998), pp. 161–207. Ross proposes that, in opposition to very imperfect choices that they currently have in relation to reproduction, women need to struggle for 'perfect choice': 'Perfect choice must involve access not only to abortion services but also to prenatal care, quality sex education, contraceptives, maternal, infant and child health services, housing and reform of the health care delivery system' (p. 200).

5. Ross, 'African-American Women and Abortion', p. 193.
6. Alex Kuczynski, 'Her Body, My Baby', *New York Times Magazine* (28 November 2008).
7. Another example of finding pleasure in forming fantasies around men who are unavailable is that of women falling in love with men on death row.

Chapter 5: Forced choice

1. Mihnea Moldoveanu and Nitin Nohria perceive decisions as terrifying because 'within them the possible is too visible in the actual for us to ignore it'. See Mihnea Moldoveanu and Nitin Nohria, *Master Passions: Emotion, Narrative, and the Development of Culture* (MIT Press, Cambridge, MA, 2002), pp. 48, 49.
2. See research presented in Daniel Kahneman, Paul Slovic and Amos Tversky (eds.) *Judgment under Uncertainty: Heuristics and Biases* (Cambridge University Press, Cambridge, 1982).
3. Peter D. Kramer, *Should You Leave?: A Psychiatrist Explores Intimacy and Autonomy – and the Nature of Advice* (Penguin, New York, 1999).

4. William Styron, *Sophie's Choice* (Jonathan Cape, London, 1979), p. 642. For a feminist analysis of the novel see Rhoda Sirlin, *William Styron's Sophie's Choice: Crime and Self-Punishment* (UMI Research Press, Ann Arbor, MI, 1990). Sirlin analyses Sophie's troubled, often submissive, relationship to men, from her father to officers in the camp and later lovers. She also looks at the gender nature of her choice and the peculiar resemblance of the sacrifice of Eve with the biblical exile of Eve from the Garden of Eden: 'Sophie knows from experience that life would be harder for Eve, indeed any female, than for Jan. Unfortunately, victimization causes self-hatred, a hatred which should more appropriately be directed towards her oppressors', p. 33.

5. Styron, *Sophie's Choice*, pp. 646, 647.

6. Luke Rhinehart, in the novel *The Dice Man* (Overlook Press, New York, 1998), plays out another devilish scenario with the idea of choice. The main character in the novel decides that he will throw a dice for every decision that he needs to make in his life, no matter what the consequences may be for him and the people around him. This ritual ends up causing complete chaos, creating a kind of psychedelic world in which chance becomes the new, mad order.

7. Sigmund Freud, 'My view of the part played by Sexuality in the Etiology of Neuroses', *The Standard Edition of the Complete Psychological Works of Sigmund Freud*, vol. VII (Hogarth Press, London, 1953), p. 275.

8. There is more on 'choice of neurosis' in Colette Soler, 'Hysteria and Obsession', in Richard Feldstein, Bruce Fink and Maire Jaanus (ed.), *Reading Seminars I and II: Lacan's Return to Freud* (SUNY Press, Albany, NY, 1996).

9. Jacques Lacan, *The Four Fundamental Concepts of Psychoanalysis*, trans. A. Sheridan, ed. J.-A. Miller (W.W. Norton and Co., New York, 1981), p. 211.

10. See Mladen Dolar, 'Beyond Interpellation', *Qui Parle*, vol. 6, no. 2, (Spring–Summer 1993), pp. 88–9.
11. See Lebrun, *Un monde sans limite*, p. 250. See also Melman, *L'homme sans gravité*.
12. Ibid.

Conclusion: Shame and the lack of social change

1. Sigmund Freud, 'Draft K – The Neuroses of Defence', in 'Extracts from the Fliess Papers', in *The Standard Edition of the Complete Psychological Works of Sigmund Freud*, vol. 1, (Hogarth Press, London, 1958), p. 224.
2. Joan Copjec, *Imagine there is no Woman: Ethics and Sublimation* (Cambridge, Mass: MIT Press, 2004), p. 128
3. *The Times* (16 June 2008); http://www.timesonline.co.uk/tol/news/politics/article4144470.ece.
4. http://articles.moneycentral.msn.com/SavingandDebt/LearnToBudget/SurvivingAndThrivingOn12000AYear.aspx.
5. http://byebyebuy.blogspot.com/2006/12/preparing-for-year-of-not-spending.html.
6. Judith Levine, *Not Buying It: My Year without Shopping* (Free Press, New York, 2006).
7. http://articles.moneycentral.msn.com/SavingandDebt/LearnToBudget/LivingPoorAnd.
8. 'Blog the Debt Away', *The New York Times* (5 March 2007); http://www.nytimes.com/2007/03/05/opinion/05mon4.html.

FURTHER READING

Benjamin, Walter, 'Capitalism as Religion,' in Walter
Benjamin, *Selected Writings: 1913–1926*, vol. I, ed. Marcus
Bullock and Michael W. Jennings (Belknap Press,
London, 1996)

Bernstein, Elizabeth, *Temporarily Yours: Intimacy,
Authenticity, and the Commerce of Sex* (University of
Chicago Press, Chicago, 2007)

Bogle, Kathleen A.: *Hooking Up: Sex, Dating, and
Relationships on Campus* (New York University Press,
New York, 2008)

Deutsch, Helen, 'Some Forms of Emotional Disturbances
and Their Relationship to Schizophrenia', in *Neuroses
and Character Types: Clinical Psychoanalytic Studies*
(International Universities Press, Madison, CT, 1965)

Dufour, Dany-Robert, *The Art of Shrinking Heads* (Polity
Press, Cambridge, 2007)

Easterbrook, Greg, *The Progress Paradox: How Life Gets
Better While People Feel Worse* (Random House, New
York, 2004)

Emerson, Ralph Waldo, *The Conduct of Life* (Houghton,
Mifflin & Co., Boston, MA, 1904)

Ferguson, Will, *Happiness™: A Novel* (Harper Perennial, New
York, 2003)

Freud, Sigmund, *The Disposition to Obsessional Neurosis: A
Contribution to the Problem of Choice of Neurosis*, vol.
XII of *The Standard Edition of the Complete Psychological
Works of Sigmund Freud*, trans. and ed. James Strachey
(Hogarth Press, London, 1958)

— *Sexuality and the Psychology of Love* (Macmillan, New
York, 1963)

Gawain, Shakti, *Living in the Light: A Guide to Personal and Planetary Transformation* (New World Library, New York, 1998)

Gawande, Atul, *Complications: A Surgeon's Notes on an Imperfect Science*, (Profile Books, London, 2003)

Gilbert, Daniel, *Stumbling on Happiness* (Alfred A. Knopf, New York, 2006)

Gladwell, Malcolm, *The Tipping Point: How Little Things Can Make a Big Difference* (Back Bay Books, New York, 2002)

— *Blink: The Power of Thinking without Thinking* (Little, Brown & Co., New York, 2005)

Gleick, James, *Faster* (Abacus, New York, 2001)

Halpern, Jake, *Fame Junkies: The Hidden Truths behind America's Favorite Addiction* (Houghton Mifflin, New York, 2007)

Harley, Willard F., *His Needs, Her Needs: Building an Affair-Proof Marriage* (Revell, Ada, MI, 2001)

Illouz, Eva, *Cold Intimacies: The Making of Emotional Capitalism* (Polity Press, Cambridge, 2007)

Jackson, Abraham, *The Pious Prentice* (Amsterdam, 16040; repr. Walter J. Johnson, Amsterdam, 1975)

Kapuściński, Ryszard, *Shah of Shahs* (Penguin, London, 2006)

Lacan, Jacques, *Ecrits: A Selection*, trans. Alan Sheridan (W.W. Norton, New York, 1977)

Laclau, Ernesto, *Emancipations* (Verso, London, 1996)

Leader, Darian, *Why Do Women Write More Letters Than They Post?* (Faber and Faber, London, 1997)

Lebrun, Jeanne-Pierre, *Un monde sans limite: essai pour une clinique psychoanalytique du social* (Erès, Paris 1997)

Legendre, Pierre, 'The Other Dimension of Law', *Cardozo Law Review*, vol. 16, no. 3–4 (1995)

McGee, Mick, *Self-Help, Inc.: Makeover Culture in American Life* (Oxford University Press, Oxford, 2005)

Melman, Charles, 'L'homme sans gravité: jouir à tout prix (Gallimard, Paris, 2005)

Miller, Jacques-Alain, and Laurent, Eric, 'The Other Who Does not Exist and His Ethical Committees', *Almanac of Psychoanalysis*, no. 1 (1998)

Millot, Catherine, *Horsexe: Essays on Transsexuality*, trans. Kenneth Hilton (Autonomedia, New York, 1989)

Niesslein, Jennifer, *Practically Perfect in Every Way* (Putnam Adult, New York, 2007)

Phaller, Robert, (ed.), *Interpassivität*, Studien über delegiertes Genießen (Springer, New York and Vienna, 2000)

Rosenthal, Edward C., *The Era of Choice: The Ability to Choose and Its Transformation of Contemporary Life* (MIT Press, Cambridge, MA, 2005).

Ross, Loretta J., 'African-American Women and Abortion', in Rickie Solinger, *Abortion Wars: A Half Century of Struggle, 1950–2000* (University of California Press, Berkeley, CA, 1998)

Russell Hochschild, Arlie, *The Commercialization of Intimate Life: Notes from Home and Work* (University of California Press, Berkeley, CA, 2003)

— *The Managed Heart: Commercialization of Human Feeling* (University of California Press, Berkeley, CA, 2003)

Salecl, Renata, *The Spoils of Freedom: Psychoanalysis and Feminism after the Fall of Socialism* (Routledge, London, 1994)

— *(Per)versions of Love and Hate* (Verso, London, 1998)

Schwartz, Barry, *The Paradox of Choice: Why More Is Less* (Harper Perennial, New York, 2005)

Sennett, Richard, *The Culture of the New Capitalism* (Yale University Press, New Haven, CT, 2007)

Sessions Stepp, Laura, *Unhooked: How Young Women Pursue Sex, Delay Love and Lose at Both* (Riverhead Books, New York, 2007)

Solinger, Rickie, *Beggars and Choosers: How the Politics of Choice Shapes Adoption, Abortion, and Welfare in the United States* (Hill and Wang, New York, 2001)

— *Pregnancy and Power: A Short History of Reproductive Politics in America*, (NYU Press, New York University Press, New York, 2005)

Stavrakakis, Jannis, *Lacan and the Political* (Routledge, London, 1999)

Styron, William, *Sophie's Choice* (Random House, New York, 1979)

Tort, Michel, *La fin du dogme paternel* (Flammarion, Paris, 2005)

Wingert, Pat, and Elkins, Sarah, 'The Incredible Shrinking Bride: How the Pressure to Look Perfect on the Big Day is Leading Some Women to Extremes', *Newsweek* (26 February 2008)

Wright, Louis B., *Middle-Class Culture in Elizabethan England* (University of North Carolina Press, Chapel Hill, NC, 1935)

Wyllie, Irvin Gordon, 'The Cult of the Self-Made Man in America (1830–1910), unpublished diss., Wisconsin, 1949

ACKNOWLEDGEMENTS

I would like to thank my agent Sarah Chalfant for her most helpful advice in shaping the outline of the book and John Stubbs for correcting my English and giving me valuable advice. The manuscript greatly benefited from Lisa Appignanesi's editing. I thank her for her patience and great comments. Sarah Caro, my editor at Profile, also gave me great feedback. I am grateful to all at Profile for their enthusiastic support of my project.

My colleagues at the Institute of Criminology at the Faculty of Law have been very supportive, providing me with their ideas and the perfect environment for writing. My colleagues at Cardozo School of Law, LSE and Birkbeck College School of Law have also contributed with their challenging ideas and valuable comments.

My son Tim gave me no choice when it came to playtime. That allowed me to get away from the book and look at the project with the humour only children are capable of.

INDEX